W9-ARR-969

Blessed is the wife whose husband offers prayers on her behalf such as those in this book. Blessed is the man who prays them, for by Case's example he will learn how to pray through a passage of Scripture for anything, not just for matters regarding his wife.
> —DONALD S. WHITNEY
> author of *Spiritual Disciplines for the Christian Life*

For husbands, or men desiring to fill God's noble calling to love their wives as Christ loved the church and gave himself up for her, *Water of the Word* provides not only a biblical framework, replete with verses to focus one's attention and catalyze one's spiritual thinking, but also beautiful prose to stir the soul of devotional prayer. More than a guidebook, it is rather a springboard to a deepening love relationship with God and with one's wife. I have used this book personally, as well as for a devotional guide for the Marriage Enrichment class here at Southern Seminary. A book to savor, reflect on, and then offer prayers from a pure heart and clear conscience.
> —WILLIAM R. CUTRER M.D.
> Gheens professor of Christian Ministry, SBTS,
> author of *Sexual Intimacy in Marriage*

Andrew Case has provided an ingenious and glorious tool for Christian husbands, one that has the potential of binding husbands and wives ever closer together while these prayers seek more intimate relationship between their wives and their God. By employing themes, principles, promises, and pleas from Scripture itself, Case has crafted hundreds of rich and meaningful prayers that any and every Christian husband can pray for his own wife. What power and insight one finds in these prayers, along with beauty and variety. Husbands here are led not only into specific prayers for their wives that focus on the central and most significant needs they have as women, but they are led also to cultivate better the habit of praying for their wives, and through this assisting the spiritual growth of those closest to them in all of life.
> —BRUCE A. WARE
> Professor of Christian Theology
> The Southern Baptist Theological Seminary

A wife of noble character is far more valuable than rubies, and a praying man is one of the primary means that God uses to develop such virtuous women. The book in your hands is of inestimable value for helping husbands persevere in this loving labor.
> —DAVID KOTTER
> Executive Director
> The Council on Biblical Manhood and Womanhood

Many believers feel paralyzed when it comes time to pray. What should be the content of our prayers? Andrew Case's prayers for a wife illustrate practically and devotionally how scripture should be the fuel for our prayers. Read, meditate, and pray!

—THOMAS R. SCHREINER
James Buchanan Professor of New Testament Interpretation
The Southern Baptist Theological Seminary

Making decisions is part and parcel of the very fabric of life: Should I have another piece of pie? Should I take my umbrella in case it rains? Should I go to this school or that one? Should I marry...? After one's decision for Christ, the decision to marry a certain individual has to be the most important decision a human being can make. It should never be made lightly nor without much forethought. Nor should it be made without prayer. And here Andrew Case's original book of prayers can be an enormous help. This volume of prayers helps orient the supplicant to desiring God's will for his life, and raises in the course of this orientation some of the key issues that need to be considered before that momentous, and altogether joyous, step of marriage. Andrew Case is to be commended for this rich labor of love that will be of benefit to so many.

—MICHAEL A. G. HAYKIN
Professor of Church History & Biblical Spirituality
The Southern Baptist Theological Seminary,
& Research Professor of Irish Baptist College,
Constituent College of Queen's University Belfast, N. Ireland

for

*a woman I have yet to meet*

Based on *The Holy Bible, English Standard Version* copyright ©2001 by Crossway Bibles, a publishing ministry of Good News Publishers. Used by permission. All rights reserved.

Andrew Case, *Water of the Word*

© 2008 by Andrew Case

All rights reserved. Any part of this publication may be shared, provided that you do not charge for or alter the content in any way.
For the free PDF please visit www.HisMagnificence.com

ISBN 978-1-43-8245-317

# Water of the Word

Husbands, love your wives, as Christ loved the church
and gave himself up for her,
that he might sanctify her,
having cleansed her
by the washing of water with the Word.
~Ephesians 5:25-26

# Contents

# Preface
## Let Us Imitate Christ as He Prays for His Bride

"Christ Jesus is the one who died—more than that, who was raised—who is at the right hand of God, who indeed is *interceding for us*" (Rom 8:34).

"He is able to save to the uttermost those who draw near to God through Him, since *He always lives to make intercession for them*" (Heb 7:25).

Christ Jesus is certainly our only hope before our great Father and righteous Judge. He sets forth the glorious example of the Husband who never tires in making intercession for His Bride until the consummation of their betrothal is complete. The wedding supper of the Lamb is what we await with breathless anticipation; to sing exuberantly, "Let us rejoice and exult and give Him the glory, for the marriage of the Lamb has come, and His Bride has made herself ready" (Rev 19:7).

Every earthly marriage has been ordained to point to the perfect union in the age to come—to reflect, albeit dimly, the intimacy and ecstasy of knowing our Saviour face to face. And if we are to be obedient to the command, "Love your wives as Christ loved the church" (Eph 5:25) we must not only show a cruciform, sacrificial love, but must also follow the precedent of continual intercession for her, pleading constantly for her sanctification (Eph 5:26). Such prayer for one's present or future wife exemplifies most sweetly the lovely ways of Christ with His Bride. There is nothing marginal or optional about the matter. For if we neglect this duty out of slothfulness or forgetfulness, the image of Christ as intercessor is marred by our foolishness and lack of discipline and wont of faith in future grace. May the LORD deal with us be it ever so severely if we, as husbands, omit this sacred opportunity of showing the love of Christ to our wives in such a tangible way; to thus increase her understanding and appreciation of her dear Saviour by our display of obedience!

If we pass over this responsibility without giving it due attention we rob ourselves and our wives of a joy and privilege full of splendid reward. Of what good is it to do everything for your wife but the best thing? To bring all manner of earthly goods before her for sustenance and honor is commendable, but to what end if you do not bring her before God? Will lifting her up by words of kindness and compliment suffice if you fail to lift her up before her Creator with supplications and thanksgivings? Why should you praise her for her beauty when you omit to exalt her Father for such matchless handiwork?

Therefore pray. Pray with all zeal and all knowledge for her. Show forth Christ to her and to the fallen world in this way. And when you do, use His Word. O what a treasure trove of prayer is afforded to us in the Bible! Seize its wisdom of petition and exultation, and learn to be a conduit of its perfect intercession, entrusting who is flesh of your flesh and bone of your bone to her Maker, the Supreme Ruler of all the world.

Not until after ten years of wavering prayers did George Mueller learn the value of praying Scripture. What follows is his description of this marvelous discovery.

The difference then between my former practice and my present one is this. Formerly, when I arose, I began to pray as soon as possible.... But what was the result? I often spent a quarter of an hour, or half an hour, or even an hour on my knees before being conscious to myself of having derived comfort, encouragement, humbling of soul, &c.; and often, after having suffered much from wandering of mind for the first ten minutes, or a quarter of an hour, or even half an hour, I only then began really to pray. I scarcely ever suffer now in this way.

My practice had been, at least for ten years previously, as an habitual thing, to give myself to prayer, after having dressed myself in the morning. Now...the first thing I did, after having asked in a few words the Lord's blessing upon His precious word, was, to begin to meditate on the word of God, searching, as it were, into every verse, to get blessing out of it.... The result I have found to be almost invariably this, that after a very few minutes my soul has been led to confession, or to thanksgiving, or to intercession, or to supplication; so that, though I did not, as it were, give myself to prayer, but to meditation, yet it turned almost immediately more or less into prayer. When thus I have been for awhile making confession, or intercession, or supplication, or have given thanks, I go on to the next words or verse, turning all, as I go on, into prayer for myself or others, as the Word may lead to it.[1]

This book is meant to be a help and guide for that kind of praying. It consists of little else than the Word of God turned "more or less into prayer." And more specifically it is a means toward one part of prayer—prayer for the good wife God has given you. We would do well to heed the council of Thomas Manton: "plead the promise of God in prayer, show Him His handwriting; God is tender of His Word."

---

[1]George Mueller, *A Narrative of Some of the Lord's Dealing with George Mueller, Written by Himself, Jehovah Magnified. Addresses by George Mueller Complete and Unabridged*, 2 vols. (Muskegon, Mich.: Dust and Ashes Publications, 2003), 1:272-273.

# *Instructions to the Reader*

## Make It Your Own

Jesus Christ is emphatically the foundation for every prayer to the Father. But the reader will notice that not all of these prayers put this precious truth into words, simply because they are meant to be springboards that launch us into other specific and more personal prayer. You are encouraged to use them as a means of centering your mind on the Bible, so that what follows in your own individual supplications will be sweetened and guided by the Word and Spirit of God.

Therefore many times I have left it to you, the reader, to be mindful that we pray in Christ's name alone. Indeed, as He Himself said, "No one comes to the Father except through me" (John 14:6). Thus we are to come to the Father in prayer always through Christ and only through Christ. Only because He is our great high priest can we "with confidence draw near to the throne of grace, that we may receive mercy and find grace to help in time of need" (Heb 4:16). And we are to give "thanks always and for everything to God the Father *in the name of our Lord Jesus Christ*" (Eph 5:20).

These prayers are also not intended to be merely read alone. To the married man I commend frequent use of these prayers *with* his wife, praying them over her from his heart, using her name. This should be the rule and not the exception, so that she is regularly reminded that Christ intercedes for her in like manner, that her husband loves her, and that the Word of God abounds with sanctifying power. For this reason a short exhortation or encouragement for her is included in many of the prayers, usually beginning with "O beloved...." Take these as occasions to lift her spirit, to strengthen her soul, to instruct her mind, to gladden her heart, to put a rock of confidence under her feet, to tenderly and humbly correct, and most of all, to point her to God as her all-satisfying joy.

As with all prayer, these must be employed in a spirit of humility, considering her better and more significant than yourself (Phil 2:3). Be ever conscious of your broken condition—that you are a sinful man who is in need of continual renewal by which you are being conformed to the image of Christ (Rom 8:29). Therefore pray strongly, as one who knows he is weak. Pray boldly, as one who knows he has no ability or confidence of himself. Pray sweetly, as one well aware of the heart within him still tinged with the bitter fruit of wickedness. And pray mindful of the truth that you are in need of just as much intercession as she. "This is the one to whom I will look: he who is humble and contrite in spirit and trembles at My word" (Isa 66:2).

The Apostle Peter warns us that it is possible to live toward our wives in such a way that our prayers become futile and unprofitable. God turns a deaf ear to the arrogant husband who dishonors his wife. "Husbands, live with your wives in an understanding way, showing honor to the woman as the weaker vessel, since they are heirs with you of the grace of life, so *that your prayers may not be hindered*" (I Pet 3:7). The unrepentant, proud husband will use this book in vain. For "God opposes the proud, but gives grace to the humble" (James 4:6).

Finally, I solemnly charge you before the God and Father of our Lord Jesus Christ to never neglect the joy and privilege of interceding for your wife. "He who finds a wife finds a good thing and obtains favor from the LORD" (Prov 18:22). And "a prudent wife is from the LORD" (Prov 19:14). God has shown marvelous favor to you, therefore pray for her with all your might while you live. Show Christ to her and to the fallen world in this way. Whatever you do for her, do not fail or forget to do the best thing. She is a gift too wonderful for you to care for alone; Sovereign Grace must guard, guide, and govern her heart and life.

*Be encouraged, dear Christian reader, with fresh earnestness to give yourself to prayer, if you can only be sure that you ask for things which are for the glory of God.*
~George Mueller

*Prayer, at its best, is the noblest, the sublimest, the most magnificent, and stupendous act that any creature of God can perform on earth or in heaven. Prayer is far too princely a life for most men. It is high, and they are low, and they cannot attain it.*
~Alexander Whyte

$O$Keeper of Your elect,

It is better to take refuge in You than to trust in man.  It is better to take refuge in You than to trust in princes.  Therefore cause my sweet wife to take refuge in You alone.  Be her strength and her song; be her great salvation.

Let her lift up the cup of salvation and call on Your Name.  Open to her the gates of righteousness, that she may enter through them and give thanks to You.  Raise her eyes to the hills to see from where her help comes.  For her help comes from You, who made heaven and earth.  Do not let her foot be moved; keep her and do not slumber.  Please keep her and neither slumber nor sleep.  Keep her from all evil; keep her life.  Keep her going out and her coming in from this time forth and forevermore.

O gift of heaven, do you know who keeps you?  The LORD is your keeper; the LORD is your shade on your right hand.  The sun shall not strike you by day, nor the moon by night.

Lord Jesus, keep my wife.  We wait eagerly for Your appearing.  Hasten the wonderful day of Your return—the wedding supper of the Lamb.  Amen (Psalm 118, 116, 121).

$\mathscr{P}$recious Provider,

Your testimonies are wonderful; therefore my soul keeps them.
May my precious wife keep them also. The unfolding of Your
word gives light; it imparts understanding to the simple. May she
open her mouth and pant, because she longs for Your
commandments. Turn to her and be gracious to her, as is Your
way with those who love Your name.

Keep steady her steps according to Your promise, let no
iniquity get dominion over her. Redeem her from man's
oppression, that she may keep Your precepts. Make Your face
shine upon her, Your beautiful servant, and teach her Your
statutes. May her eyes shed streams of tears, because people do
not keep Your law (Psalm 119).

*A man cannot live unless he takes his breath, nor can the soul, unless*
*it breathes forth its desires to God.* ~Thomas Watson

*O*LORD God of heaven,

The great and awesome God who keeps covenant and steadfast love with those who love Him and keep His commandments, let Your ear be attentive and Your eyes open, to hear the prayer of Your servant that I now pray before You day and night for my beautiful wife. Grant her continual patience and forbearance to live with me, a wicked husband. For I have sinned against You; I have acted very corruptly against You by forsaking my responsibility to lead my home in righteousness and the fear of You; I have not kept Your commandments, Your statutes, or the rules that You commanded Your servant Moses.

Give her boldness and wisdom to rebuke and exhort me when I am unfaithful to Your Word, when I neglect prayer, fail to redeem the time, speak carelessly, walk foolishly, fail to hope in You, seek great things for myself, become anxious about tomorrow. Do not let her cease praying for me when I am beset with the fear of man, the cares of the world, or the love of money. May she never lose confidence that, in spite of my many iniquities and shortcomings, I am Your servant whom You have redeemed by Your great power and by Your strong hand.

O Lord, let Your ear be attentive to the prayer of Your servant, and to the prayers of my wife who delights to fear Your name, and give success to her today, and grant her mercy (Nehemiah 1).

$\mathcal{M}$erciful Master,

Look on her affliction and deliver her, and let her not forget Your law. Plead her cause and redeem her; give her life according to Your promise! Salvation is far from the wicked, for they do not seek Your statutes. Great is Your mercy, O LORD; give her life according to Your rules.

Even when her persecutors and adversaries are many, let her not swerve from Your testimonies. May she look at the faithless with pity, because they do not keep Your commands. Consider how she loves Your precepts! Give her life according to Your steadfast love. The sum of Your word is truth, and every one of Your righteous rules endures forever (Psalm 119).

*To begin the day with prayer is but a formality unless it go on in prayer, unless for the rest of it we pray in deed what we began in word. One has said that while prayer is the day's best beginning it must not be like the handsome title-page of a worthless book.* ~ P. T. Forsyth

$\mathcal{S}$overeign Preserver,

Let my dear wife stand up and bless You our God from everlasting to everlasting. Blessed be Your glorious name, which is exalted above all blessing and praise. You are the LORD, You alone. You have made *her*. You have made heaven, the heaven of heavens, with all their host, the earth and all that is on it, the seas and all that is in them; and You preserve all of them; and the host of heaven worships You.

Thank You for preserving my wife, for keeping her as Your chosen, for directing her steps on the narrow way. Please continue to preserve her life! For You are the LORD, the God who chose her and brought her out of darkness and made her heart faithful before You. Thank You that You have kept the promises that are hers in Christ Jesus, for You are righteous. I praise You that You are a God ready to forgive, gracious and merciful, slow to anger and abounding in steadfast love, and have not departed from her. Even when she strays and her heart grows dull, You in Your great mercies have not forsaken her. Therefore, keep on making a name for Yourself through her, and instruct her with Your good Spirit. Amen (Nehemiah 9).

*T*hou Great Being who made and rules the world,

Put Your Spirit in my wife with perfect power and bear His fruits from her life. May she be a loving woman; a joyful, peaceful woman; a patient, kind, good wife. Make her soul and actions abound with faithfulness, gentleness, and self-control, for against such things there is no law. By Christ Jesus crucify her flesh with its passions and desires.

Let her not grow weary in doing good, for in due season she will reap if she does not give up. And may she never boast except in the cross of our Lord Jesus Christ, by which the world has been crucified to her, and she to the world (Galatians 5 & 6).

*Prayer seem'd to be natural to me; as the breath, by which the inward burnings of my heart had vent.* ~Jonathan Edwards

reat God,

May my beautiful wife be a woman inclined to pour herself out for the hungry and satisfy the desire of the afflicted, so that her light will rise in the darkness and her gloom be as the noonday. Then guide her continually and satisfy her desire in scorched places. Make her bones strong, so that she is like a watered garden, like a spring of water, whose waters do not fail.

May she be radiant; her heart thrilled to say, "I will greatly rejoice in the LORD; my soul shall exult in my God, for He has clothed me with the garments of salvation; He has covered me with the robe of righteousness." Make her count the garments of salvation as sufficient clothing, valued by her as more precious and worthy of care than the adornments of a queen. May her robes of righteousness be ever prevalent, outshining worldly dress. Amen (Isaiah 58 & 61).

$\mathcal{R}$ighteous are You, O LORD, and right are Your rules.

You have appointed Your testimonies in righteousness and in faithfulness. May zeal consume my wife when her foes forget Your words. Your promise is well tried; may she love it. Even when she is small and despised, let her not forget Your precepts. Your righteousness is righteous forever, and Your law is true. When trouble and anguish find her out, make Your commandments her delight. Your testimonies are righteous forever; give her understanding that she may live.

With my whole heart I cry for her; answer me, O LORD! Cause her to keep Your statutes. I call to You; save her, that she may observe Your testimonies. I rise before dawn and cry for help; may she hope in Your words. Awaken her eyes before the watches of the night, that she may meditate on Your promise. Hear my voice according to Your steadfast love; O LORD, according to Your justice give her life. When they draw near who persecute her with evil purpose, who are far from Your law, assure her that You are near, O LORD, and all Your commandments are true. Long have I known from Your testimonies that You have founded them forever (Psalm 119).

*What makes a heart upright and what makes prayers pleasing to God is a felt awareness of our tremendous need for mercy.* ~John Piper

$\mathcal{My}$ Gracious Master,

Cause my delightful wife to work out her own salvation with fear and trembling, knowing all the while that it is You who work in her, both to will and to work for Your good pleasure.

May she rejoice in You always, and let her reasonableness be known to everyone. Please let her not be anxious about anything, but in everything by prayer and supplication with thanksgiving may she make known her requests to You. And all this so that Your peace, which surpasses all understanding, will guard her precious heart and mind in Christ Jesus.

Finally Father, make her think on whatever is true, whatever is honorable, whatever is just, whatever is pure, whatever is lovely, whatever is commendable, on anything of excellence, and anything worthy of praise. Through Your Son and for Your glory I ask these things. Amen (Philippians 2 & 4).

*Couples who do not pray are as badly off as those who stop sleeping together. Like lovemaking, prayer requires, in a sense, taking off the clothes, removing the shoes to touch holy ground.* ~Mike Mason

# Heavenly Father,

As for me, my prayer is to You. At an acceptable time, O God, in the abundance of Your steadfast love answer me in Your saving faithfulness. And my prayer is this: deliver my wife from sinking in the mire of sin; let her be delivered from the deep waters of vanity. Let not the flood sweep over her, or the deep swallow her up, or the pit of despair close its mouth over her. Answer me, O LORD, for Your steadfast love is good; according to Your abundant mercy turn to her. Draw near to her soul, redeem her; ransom her because of her frailty.

When she is afflicted and in pain, let Your salvation, O God, set her on high! Then may she praise Your Name with a song, and magnify You with thanksgiving. May she seek You, and rejoice and be glad in You!

O beloved, because we love His salvation, let us say together evermore, "God is great!" Hasten to us, O God! You are our help and our deliverer; O LORD, do not delay! Save us for Your marvelous Name (Psalm 69 & 70).

essed God,

Although princes may persecute her without cause, may my precious wife's heart stand in awe of Your words. Might she, by the power of Your Spirit, rejoice at Your word like one who finds great spoil. Make her hate and abhor falsehood, but love Your law. Cause her to praise You seven times a day for Your righteous rules. Great peace have those who love Your law; nothing can make them stumble. May she hope for Your salvation, O LORD, and do Your commandments. Cause her soul to keep Your testimonies and love them exceedingly. Help her to keep Your precepts and testimonies, for all her ways are before You.

Let my cry come before You, O LORD; give her understanding according to Your word! Let my plea come before You; deliver her according to Your word. May her lips pour forth praise, for You teach her Your statutes. May her tongue sing of Your word, for all Your commandments are right. Let Your hand be ready to help her, for she has chosen Your precepts. Create in her a longing for Your salvation, O LORD, and a delight in Your law. Let her soul live and praise You, and let Your rules help her. When she goes astray like a lost sheep, seek her, Your servant, for she does not forget Your commandments. Amen (Psalm 119).

*You often feel that your prayers scarcely reach the ceiling; but, oh, get into this humble spirit by considering how good the Lord is, and how evil you all are, and then prayer will mount on wings of faith to heaven. The sigh, the groan of a broken heart, will soon go through the ceiling up to heaven, aye, into the very bosom of God.* ~Charles Simeon

*Even skeptical Dan prayed, his skepticism falling away from him like a discarded garment in this valley of the shadow, which sifts out hearts and tries souls, until we all, grown-up or children, realize our weakness, and, finding that our own puny strength is as a reed shaken in the wind, creep back humbly to the God we have vainly dreamed we could do without.* ~L.M. Montgomery

ord Jesus,

It is by Your undying death and willing sacrifice that I come to my Father who has loved me with an everlasting love for no reason but His own purpose and glory. And so I ask, LORD and Sovereign, that my wife would be blessed because her way is blameless; that she would walk in the law of the LORD! Cause her to keep Your testimonies and seek You with her whole heart, doing no wrong but walking in Your ways.

May she keep Your precepts diligently for love of Your great Name. Oh, that her ways may be steadfast in keeping Your statutes! May her blessed eyes be fixed unswervingly on all Your commandments. Please ignite such joy in her that she must praise You with an upright heart when she learns Your righteous rules. And cause her to keep Your statutes; do not utterly forsake her!

Keep her way pure by teaching her to guard it according to Your word. I ask that she be made into such a woman who seeks You with her whole heart, crying out, "Let me not wander from Your commandments." May she store up Your word in her heart that she might not sin against You. Blessed are You, O LORD; teach her Your statutes!

May her lips be not only consecrated to me, but all the more to declaring the rules of Your mouth. And with all my might I plead that in the way of Your testimonies she would delight as much as in all riches...as much as in all friends...more so than any worldly lust and pleasure. Quicken her mind to meditate on Your precepts and fix her eyes on Your ways.  I desire little else for her than that she delight in Your statutes and not forget Your word (Psalm 119).

*How much my father's prayers at this time impressed me I can never explain, nor could any stranger understand.  When, on his knees and all of us kneeling around him in Family Worship, he poured out his whole soul with tears for the conversion of the Heathen world to the service of Jesus, and for every personal and domestic need, we all felt as if in the presence of the living Savior, and learned to know and love him as our Divine friend.*  ~James C. Paton

*I*neffable Lover,

Only by the Cross do I bring these prayers to You for my treasured wife. Do not let her adorning be merely external—the braiding of hair, the wearing of gold, or the putting on of clothing—but let her adorning be the hidden person of the heart with the imperishable beauty of a gentle and quiet spirit, which in Your sight is very precious.

Give her unity of mind, sympathy, sisterly love, a tender heart, and humility. The end of all things is at hand; therefore let her be self-controlled and sober-minded for the sake of her prayers. Above all, keep her loving others earnestly, since love covers a multitude of sins.

As she has received a gift, may she use it to serve others, as a good steward of Your varied grace. When she speaks, let it be as one who speaks the oracles of God; when she serves, as one who serves by the strength that You supply—in order that in everything You may be glorified through Jesus Christ. To You belong glory and dominion forever and ever. Amen (I Peter 3 & 4).

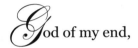od of my end,

Deal bountifully with my wife, Your servant, that she may live
and keep Your word. And this I ask with importunate reverence:
open her eyes, that she may behold wondrous things out of Your
law. O that her eyes would sparkle with pure and deep delight
when Your Truth is shone into them out of grace. For she is a
mere sojourner on this earth; hide not Your commandments from
her!

Consume her soul with longing for Your rules at all times, for
You rebuke the insolent, accursed ones, who wander from Your
commandments. Take away from her scorn and contempt, for she
has kept Your testimonies. Cause her to meditate on Your statutes
even when princes sit plotting against her. May it be readily on
her lips, "Your testimonies are my delight; they are my
counselors."

When her soul clings to the dust please give her life according
to Your word! When she tells You of her ways, answer her; teach
her Your statutes! Make her understand the way of Your precepts
and meditate on Your wondrous works.

When her soul melts away for sorrow—for she *will* be well-
acquainted with grief if she is Yours—strengthen her according to
Your word! She is ever surrounded by false ways in this age; teach
her Your law! She has chosen the way of faithfulness; may she set
Your rules ever before her. When she clings to Your testimonies,

O LORD, let her not be put to shame! Enlarge her heart so that she may run in the way of Your commandments! (Psalm 119).

*How easily we convince ourselves that we are praying to the Lord when in reality we are locked in our own thoughts. We need to ask: If I'm happy, am I really rejoicing in Him, or am I rejoicing in my own self-satisfaction? If I'm worried or afraid, am I truly and humbly asking Him for help, or is my mind busy trying to work out some plan (however spiritual it may seem) for getting myself out of trouble.*
~Mike Mason

$\mathcal{A}$mighty God,

Please teach my wonderful wife the way of Your statutes; may she keep it to the end, as her reward. Give her understanding that she may keep Your law and observe it with her whole heart. Lead her in the path of Your commandments, because she delights in it—O Father, cause her to delight in Your path!

Incline her heart to Your testimonies, and not to selfish gain! Turn her eyes from looking at worthless things; and give her life in Your ways. Confirm to her Your promise, that she may fear You—fear You with every fiber of her beautiful heart. Turn away the reproach that she dreads, for Your rules are good. Behold, may she long for Your precepts; in Your righteousness give her life!

Let Your steadfast love come to her, O LORD, Your salvation according to Your promise; then shall she have an answer for anyone who taunts her, for she trusts in Your word. Sovereign LORD, may she trust the Bible with all her might! And take not the word of truth utterly out of her mouth, for her hope is in Your rules. May she keep Your law continually, forever and ever, and may she walk in a wide place, for she has sought Your precepts.

Make her also speak of Your testimonies before kings and be not put to shame, for she finds her delight in Your commandments, which she loves. May she lift up her hands toward Your commandments, and meditate on Your statutes. Amen, come Lord Jesus (Psalm 119).

$\mathcal{F}$ather of Wisdom,

Let me never cease to pray for my beautiful wife, asking that she may be filled with the knowledge of Your will in all spiritual wisdom and understanding, so as to walk in a manner worthy of You, bearing fruit in every good work and increasing in the knowledge of You. May she be strengthened with all power, according to Your glorious might, for all endurance and patience with joy, giving thanks to You, who have qualified her to share in the inheritance of the saints in light.

Do you remember, my beloved, that He has delivered you from the domain of darkness and transferred you to the kingdom of His beloved Son, in whom you have redemption, the forgiveness of sin? Yes, praise Him with me for His marvelous grace!

O LORD God, make her continue in the faith, stable and steadfast, not shifting from the hope of the gospel that she heard, which has been proclaimed in all creation under heaven. Keep her! Keep her! Keep her in the love of Christ. Amen (Colossians 1).

*Anyone who would have power in prayer must be merciless in dealing with his own sins.* ~R.A. Torrey

 iver of all,

Remember Your word to Your servant, in which You have
made me hope. May my wife's comfort in her affliction be this:
that Your promise gives her life. The insolent might utterly deride
her, but do not let her turn away from Your law. When she thinks
of Your rules from of old, let her take comfort, O LORD. O that hot
indignation might seize her because of the wicked, who forsake
Your law. And I ask that Your statutes would be her songs in the
house of her sojourning. Cause her to remember Your Name in
the night, O LORD, and keep Your law. This blessing has fallen to
her, that she has kept Your precepts.

When she kneels to pray, let her say, "You are my portion; I
promise to keep Your words." I entreat Your favor with all my
heart; be gracious to her according to Your promise. When she
thinks on her ways, let her turn her feet to Your testimonies; may
she hasten and not delay to keep Your commandments. Though
the cords of the wicked ensnare her, allow her not to forget Your
law. And this I plead with fervent hope—that at midnight she
would rise to praise You, because of Your righteous rules, for only
by a miracle of Your hand will it be so with her. Make her the
companion of all who fear You, of those who keep Your precepts.
The earth, O LORD, is full of Your steadfast love; teach her Your
statutes! (Psalm 119).

God,

Blessed is the woman who fears You, who greatly delights in Your commandments! Please continue to mold my winsome wife into such a woman.

Make light dawn in the darkness for her; You are gracious, merciful, and righteous. Grant that she deal generously and lend, conducting her affairs with justice. Let her never be moved; remember her forever.

May she be not afraid of bad news, but make her heart firm, trusting in You. Give her a steady heart, so that from the rising of the sun to its setting she will praise Your glorious Name.

O sweet bone of my bone, trust in the LORD! He is your help and your shield. O wonderful flesh of my flesh, trust in the LORD! He is your help and your shield. You who fear the LORD, trust in Him! He is your help and your shield. May you be blessed by the LORD, who made heaven and earth! We will bless You, O God, from this time forth and forevermore. Praise the LORD! (Psalm 112, 113, 115).

*We are not so foolish as to think we can learn a trade without the diligent use of helps. Shall we think that we may become spiritually skilful and wise in the understanding of this mystery without making any real effort to use the helps God has given us? The most important of them is fervent prayer. Pray with Paul that 'the eyes of your understanding may be enlightened to behold' the glory of God in Christ. Pray that the 'God of our Lord Jesus Christ, the Father of glory, may give to you the spirit of wisdom and revelation in the knowledge of him.' Fill your minds with spiritual thoughts of Christ. Lazy souls do not get the tiniest sight of this glory. The 'lion in the way' deters them from making the slightest effort.* ~John Owen

$O$ Great Upholder and Proprietor of all things,

Please deal with my wife, Your sweet servant, according to Your word. Teach her good judgment and knowledge, for she believes Your commandments. Even though she has gone astray before her affliction, assist her now to keep Your word. You are good and do good; teach her Your statutes. Although the insolent may smear her with lies, help her keep Your precepts with her whole heart; their heart is unfeeling, but she delights in Your law.

It is good for her to be afflicted, that she might learn Your statutes. And if this be what sanctifies her further, please bring suffering to her again. The law of Your mouth is better to me than thousands of gold and silver pieces. Your hands have made and fashioned her; give her understanding that she may learn Your commandments. And praise be to the Creator of heaven and earth for fashioning such infinite loveliness in her! Those who fear You shall see her and rejoice, because she has hoped in Your word. O that such a lofty thought might be true! I know, O LORD, that Your rules are righteous, and that in faithfulness You afflict her. Let Your steadfast love comfort her according to Your promise to Your servant.

Let Your mercy go to her, that she may live; for Your law is her delight. Let the insolent be put to shame, because they have wronged her with falsehood; as for her, may she meditate on Your precepts. Let those who fear You turn to her, that they may know Your testimonies. May her heart be blameless in Your statutes, that she may not be put to shame! Amen (Psalm 119).

*O*timeless Light of lights, Eternal Father,

Make my wife's sweet soul long for Your salvation; may she hope in Your word. Be the cause of her eyes longing for Your promise; of her asking, "When will You comfort me?" Let her seek the deepest of comfort in Your steadfast love and faithfulness. When she becomes like a wineskin in the smoke, let her not forget Your statutes. How long must Your servant endure? When will You judge those who persecute her? The insolent have dug pitfalls for her; they do not live according to Your law. All Your commandments are sure; they persecute her with falsehood; help her! When they have almost made an end of her on earth, let her not forsake Your precepts. In Your steadfast love give her life, that she may keep the testimonies of Your mouth.

Forever, O LORD, Your word is firmly fixed in the heavens. Your faithfulness endures to all generations; You have established the earth and it stands fast. By Your appointment they stand this day, for all things are Your servants. If Your law is not made to be my wife's delight, she will surely perish in her affliction. Oh, that she would never forget Your precepts, for by them You have given her life. She is Yours, save her, for she has sought Your precepts. When the wicked lie in wait to destroy her, may she consider Your testimonies. I have seen a limit to all perfection, but Your commandment is exceedingly broad. Give her life in Your ways. Amen. Come, Lord Jesus (Psalm 119).

*It is very apparent from the word of God, that he is wont often to try the faith and patience of his people, when crying to him for some great and important mercy, by withholding the mercy sought, for a season; and not only so, but at first to cause an increase of dark appearances. And yet he, without fail, at last succeeds those who continue instant in prayer, with all perseverance, and will not let him go except he blesses.*
~Jonathan Edwards

*What a blessed thing is the marriage of two believers, of one hope, one discipline, servants of the same Master! . . . Together they offer up their prayers - together they lie in the dust, and keep their fasts, teaching each other, exhorting each other, bearing up each other. They are together in God's Church, together at God's feast, together in straits, persecutions, consolations; freely the sick are visited and the indigent supported; there are alms without trouble; sacrifices without scruple; daily unimpeded diligence. Christ sees it and rejoices.* ~Tertullian

*C*hangeless God,

May my beautiful wife never forget all Your benefits. Help me to remind her relentlessly of the One who forgives all her iniquity, who heals all her diseases, who redeems her life from the pit, who crowns her with steadfast love and mercy, who satisfies her with good so that her youth is renewed like the eagle's. Please work righteousness and justice for her when she is oppressed. Make known Your ways to her, Your acts to Your precious daughter.

O gift of heaven, hear again of our marvelous God! The LORD is merciful and gracious, slow to anger and abounding in steadfast love. He will not always chide, nor will He keep His anger forever. He does not deal with you according to your sins, nor repay you according to your iniquities. For as high as the heavens are above the earth, so great is His steadfast love toward those who fear Him; as far as the east is from the west, so far does He remove your transgressions from you.

O LORD, as a father shows compassion to his children, please show compassion to her. For You know her frame; You remember that she is dust.

Come quickly, Lord Jesus! Amen, we long and wait for You (Psalm 103).

*There is nothing in which we need to take so many lessons as in prayer. There is nothing of which we are so utterly ignorant when we first begin; there is nothing in which we are so helpless.* ~Alexander Whyte

$\mathscr{S}$overeign Creator and Sustainer,

Oh how I love Your law! May it be my wife's meditation all the day. Your commandment makes her wiser than her enemies, for it is ever with her. Grant her more understanding than all her teachers by making Your testimonies her meditation. May she understand more than the aged, because she keeps Your precepts. Assist her to hold back her feet from every evil way, in order to keep Your word. May she not turn aside from Your rules, for You have taught her. Please cause her to say, "How sweet are Your words to my taste, sweeter than honey to my mouth!" Through Your precepts make her get understanding, and so hate every false way.

Your word is a lamp to her feet and a light to her path. May she swear an oath and confirm it, to keep Your righteous rules. When she is severely afflicted please give her life, O LORD, according to Your word! Accept her free offerings of praise, O LORD, and teach her Your rules. Though she may hold her life in her hand continually, let her not forget Your law. When the wicked lay a snare for her, may she not stray from Your precepts. Make Your testimonies her heritage forever, and the joy of her heart. Incline her heart to perform Your statutes forever, to the end. Amen (Psalm 119).

$\mathcal{S}$weet Sustainer and Rock of Salvation,

I do not ask that You take my dear wife out of the world, but that You keep her from the evil one. Sanctify her in the truth; Your word is truth. Father, I desire that she also, whom You have given to Christ, may be with Him where He is, to see His glory that You have given Him because You loved Him before the foundation of the world.

I give thanks to You always for my lovely wife because of Your grace that has been given her in Christ Jesus, and I ask that in every way she may be enriched in You in all speech and all knowledge—even that the testimony about Christ might be confirmed in her—so that she will not be lacking in any spiritual gift, as she waits for the revealing of our Lord Jesus Christ, who will sustain her to the end, guiltless in the day of Christ.

O God, be the source of her life in Christ Jesus, whom You made her wisdom and her righteousness and sanctification and redemption. Therefore, let her boast solely in You. For the display of Your wonderful winsomeness, Amen (John 17 & I Corinthians 1).

*Desire gives fervor to prayer. The soul cannot be listless when some great desire fixes and inflames it...Strong desires make strong prayers...The neglect of prayer is the fearful token of dead spiritual desires...There can be no true praying without desire.* ~E. M. Bounds

$\mathcal{O}$Father of my dearest Lord Jesus,

May my wife hate the double-minded, but love Your law. Be her hiding place, and her shield; make her hope in Your word. Cause evildoers to depart from her, that she may keep the commandments of her God. Uphold her according to Your promise, that she may live, and let her not be put to shame in her hope! Hold her up, that she may be safe and have regard for Your statutes continually! You spurn all who go astray from Your statutes, for their cunning is in vain. All the wicked of the earth You discard like dross, therefore may she love Your testimonies. Might she say in her heart, "My flesh trembles for fear of You, and I am afraid of Your judgments."

She has done what is just and right; do not leave her to her oppressors. Give her a pledge of good; let not the insolent oppress her. May her eyes long for Your salvation and for the fulfillment of Your righteous promise. Deal with my wife, Your servant, according to Your steadfast love, and teach her Your statutes. She is Your servant; give her understanding, that she may know Your testimonies! It is time for You to act, for Your law has been broken. Therefore, may she cry in her heart, "I love Your commandments above gold, above fine gold. Therefore I consider all Your precepts to be right; I hate every false way." Amen, Come Lord Jesus (Psalm 119).

$\mathcal{O}$ur Father in heaven,

Hallowed be Your Name. Please keep Your Name holy in the life of my beautiful wife. Cause her to consider it reverently in her mind and heart, treating it as sacred by her words and conduct.

May Your kingdom come, and may she long for the day of Your fullness far more than anything else in this life. Stir her heart to seek first Your kingdom.

Your will be done on earth as it is in heaven. Perform Your good pleasure in her—use her as a vessel to magnify the beauty of Your Son. Give her this day her daily bread, providing for her physical needs, for You are a loving, merciful Father who gives good gifts to His children. Teach her to trust You, being not anxious about whether she will have enough for tomorrow.

Forgive her her debts, as she also forgives her debtors. Forgive her when she falls short of Your glory. And form in her a pardoning heart, forbearing in everything.

Lead her not into temptation, but deliver her from evil. Rescue her from the deceitfulness of sin. By Your undeserved mercy keep her heart from being darkened and led into foolishness. For Yours is the kingdom, the power, and the glory forever! Amen (Matthew 6).

*Giving God good advice, and abusing the devil isn't praying.*
~L.M. Montgomery

*My* Exceeding Joy,

Help me never cease to give thanks for my dear wife, remembering her in my prayers, that You, the God of my Lord Jesus Christ, the Father of glory, may give her a spirit of wisdom and of revelation in the knowledge of You, having the eyes of her heart enlightened, that she may know what is the hope to which You have called her, what are the riches of Your glorious inheritance in the saints, and what is the immeasurable greatness of Your power toward us who believe, according to the working of Your great might.

O LORD, she cannot know and delight in the mystery and beauty of Your gospel unless Your Spirit intervenes, bringing about fruit in her for righteousness. For this reason I bow my knees before You, Father, from whom every family in heaven and on earth is named, that according to the riches of Your glory You may strengthen her with power through Your Spirit in her inner being, so that Christ may dwell in her heart through faith—that she, being rooted and grounded in love, may have strength to comprehend with all the saints what is the breadth and length and height and depth, and to *know* the love of Christ that surpasses knowledge, that she may be filled with all of Your fullness.

Now to You who are able to do far more abundantly than all that we ask or think, according to the power at work within us, to You be glory in the church and in Christ Jesus throughout all generations, forever and ever Amen (Ephesians 1 & 3).

*M*erciful LORD,

I know that it is Your good pleasure to give of Yourself to those who ask; therefore I pray that my precious wife's delight would be in Your law. May she meditate on it day and night. Teach her what it is to serve You with fear and rejoice with trembling.

O LORD, be a shield about her, her glory, and the lifter of her head. Assist her to put her trust in You so that her heart exults, saying, "You have put more joy in my heart than they have when their grain and wine abound." In peace make her both lie down and sleep; for You alone, O LORD, make her dwell in safety. Lead her, O LORD, in Your righteousness because of her enemies; make Your way straight before her. Let her take refuge in You and rejoice; let her ever sing for joy, and spread Your protection over her, that she who loves Your Name may exult in You.

For You bless the righteous, O LORD; You cover her with favor as with a shield. May she give to You the thanks due to Your righteousness, and sing praise to Your Name, Most High.

O beloved, give thanks to the LORD with your whole heart; recount all of His wonderful deeds! Be glad and exult in God; sing praise to His Name, the Most High. For those who know Your Name, O LORD, put their trust in You, for You have not forsaken those who seek You.

Remind her that she is but a woman, wholly dependent upon You for life and breath and everything else. I commit her to You. Amen (Psalm 2, 4, 5, 9).

*T*hou Great I Am,

You are righteous; You love righteous deeds; the upright shall behold Your face. Therefore cause my lovely wife to walk uprightly so that she might do what she was made for—behold Your wonderful face! May she trust in Your steadfast love; may her heart rejoice in Your salvation. And then let her sing to You, because You have dealt bountifully with her. Again I ask that she be constrained to walk blamelessly and do what is right and speak the truth in her heart.

O that she would say and continue to say to You, "You are my Lord; I have no good apart from You. You are my chosen portion and my cup; You hold my lot." May she set You always before her; trusting that because You are at her right hand, she shall not be shaken. Please make known to her the path of life; that in Your presence there is fullness of joy; at Your right hand are pleasures evermore.

Wondrously show Your steadfast love to her, O Savior of those who seek refuge from their adversaries at Your right hand. Keep her as the apple of Your eye; hide her in the shadow of Your wings. As for her, may she behold Your face in righteousness; when she awakes, may she be satisfied with Your likeness. Praise the LORD! (Psalm 11, 13, 16, 17).

*No prayer is more powerful than the prayer of powerlessness, of littleness, of not knowing. Isn't this what it means to be poor in spirit?*
~Mike Mason

*O*triune God,

I love You, O LORD, my strength. May You be to my winsome wife her rock and her fortress and her deliverer, her God, her rock, in whom she takes refuge, her shield, and the horn of her salvation, her stronghold. You alone are worthy to be praised.

By Your mercy bring her out into a broad place; rescue her, because You delight in her. Put all Your rules before her, and may she never put Your statutes away from her. For it is You who light her lamp; O LORD my God, lighten her darkness. Make her abide in this precious promise: "This God—His way is perfect; the word of the LORD proves true; He is a shield for all those who take refuge in Him."

Give her the shield of Your salvation, and with Your right hand support her, and with Your gentleness make her great. With Your perfect law, O LORD, revive her soul. With Your sure testimony make her wise. By Your right precepts cause her heart to rejoice. And may Your pure commandment enlighten her eyes.

Keep her, Your servant, also from presumptuous sins; let them not have dominion over her! Let the words of her mouth and the meditation of her heart be pleasing in Your sight, O LORD, my Rock and my Redeemer (Psalm 18 & 19).

$\mathcal{I}$nfinite Father,

It is my plea by the Name of Christ, that You hear me on behalf
of my sweet wife. Since she is one of Your holy and beloved
chosen, then put on her compassion, kindness, humility,
meekness, and patience. And if one has a complaint against her,
let her forgive as You have forgiven her. And above all these put
on her love, which binds everything together in perfect harmony.
And let the peace of Christ rule in her heart, to which indeed she
was called. And may she be thankful. Let the word of Christ dwell
in her richly, as she teaches and admonishes others in all wisdom,
singing psalms and hymns and spiritual songs, with thankfulness
in her heart to You. And whatever she does, in word or deed, may
everything be in the Name of the Lord Jesus, giving thanks to You,
her Father, through Him.

O beloved, continue steadfastly in prayer, being watchful in it
with thanksgiving. I commit you to our dearest and fairest Lord
Jesus. He will sustain you. Amen (Colossians 3 & 4).

*A*l-sufficient King,

May You answer my dear wife in the day of trouble! May Your great Name, God of Jacob, protect her! Grant her heart's desire and fulfill all her plans! May she shout for joy over Your salvation, and in the name of her God set up her banners! May You fulfill all her petitions.

Some trust in chariots and some in horses, but let *her* trust in the name of the LORD her God. Make her glad with the joy of Your presence. Be exalted, O LORD, in Your strength! Let her sing and praise Your power.

When trouble is near and there is none to help, be not far from her. For You, O LORD, are her shepherd; she shall not want. Please make her to lie down in green pastures. Lead her beside still waters. Restore her soul. And by grace, lead her in paths of righteousness for Your Name's sake.

Even when she walks through the valley of the shadow of death, let her fear no evil, for You are with her; with Your rod and Your staff comfort her. May goodness and mercy follow her all the days of her life, that she may dwell in Your house forever (Psalm 20 & 23).

*For my part, if I cannot pray, I would rather know it, and groan over my soul's barrenness till the Lord shall again visit me with fruitfulness of devotion.* ~Charles Spurgeon

$\mathcal{L}$ife-giving God,

O that the breathtaking wife You have provided for me would have clean hands and a pure heart! Guard her so that she does not lift up her soul to what is false or swear deceitfully. Guide her so that she might receive blessings from You and righteousness from the God of her salvation. Cause her to seek You, to seek the face of the God of Jacob.

To You, O LORD, I lift up her soul. O my God, in You I trust; let her not be put to shame; let not her enemies exult over her. Make her to know Your ways, O LORD; teach her Your paths. Lead her in Your truth and teach her, for You are the God of her salvation; for You she waits all the day long.

According to Your steadfast love remember her, for the sake of Your goodness, O LORD! Lead her in humility and what is right; teach her Your way. Instruct her in the way You should choose.

Your friendship, O LORD, is for those who fear You, and You make known to them Your covenant. And so I ask importunately that You would fill her with the fear of You so that she might be Your friend.

Cause her eyes to be ever toward You. Turn to her and be gracious to her when she is lonely and afflicted. O guard her soul and deliver her! Let her not be put to shame, for she takes refuge in You. May integrity and uprightness preserve her, for she waits for You (Psalm 24 & 25).

ord of Heaven,

Cause my wife—the delight of my eyes—to walk in integrity. May she trust in You without wavering. Prove her, O LORD, and try her; test her heart and her mind. Manifest Your steadfast love before her eyes that she may walk in Your faithfulness. Redeem her and be gracious to her.

You are her light and her salvation; whom shall she fear? You are the stronghold of her life; of whom shall she be afraid?

O LORD, I love how You have made her Your habitation and a place where Your glory dwells. I pray that she would earnestly say with the Psalmist, "One thing have I asked of the LORD, that will I seek after: that I may dwell in the house of the LORD all the days of my life, to gaze upon the beauty of the LORD and to inquire in his temple."

Let her heart also cry, "Your face, LORD, do I seek." Hide not Your face from her. Cast her not off; forsake her not, O God of my salvation!

O my exquisite beloved, wait for the LORD; be strong, and let your heart take courage; wait for the LORD! (Psalm 26 & 27).

*Prayer often avails where everything else fails.* ~R.A. Torrey

*S*overeign Commander of the universe,

You are my wife's only true strength and shield; in You may her heart trust and be helped; let her heart exult, and with her song give thanks to You. You are the strength of Your people; be the saving refuge of my precious wife. May You give strength to her!

When she is mourning, turn it into dancing; loose her sackcloth and clothe her with gladness, that her glory may sing Your praise and not be silent. O LORD my God, I will give thanks to You forever!

In You, O LORD, may she take refuge; let her never be put to shame; in Your righteousness deliver her! Cause her to rejoice and be glad in Your steadfast love. Make Your face shine on her; save her in Your steadfast love!

O my beloved earthly treasure, the LORD preserves the faithful; be strong and let your heart take courage, you who wait for the LORD!

Keep her, Father; I commit her wholly to Your Hand (Psalm 28, 30, 31).

$\mathcal{O}$Fountain of all good,

Instruct my cherished wife and teach her in the way she should go; counsel her with Your eye upon her.

May Your steadfast love surround her because she trusts in You. Make her glad in You; make her rejoice as a righteous one, shouting for joy as one upright in heart!

Let all the earth fear the LORD; let all the inhabitants of the world stand in awe of You! For You spoke, and she came to be; You commanded, and she stands firm. Behold, how good it is that Your eye is on those who fear You, on those who hope in Your steadfast love. O that her soul would wait for You; be her help and her shield. Together, may our hearts be glad in You, because we trust in Your holy Name. Let Your steadfast love, O LORD, be upon us, even as we hope in You.

Cause her to bless You at all times; may Your praise continually be in her mouth. Let her say, "My soul makes its boast in the LORD; let the humble hear and be glad."

Dearest among women, oh magnify the LORD with me, and let us exalt His Name together! (Psalm 32, 33, 34).

$\mathscr{S}$earcher of hearts,

I ask with reverent joy and trembling that my wife—my incomparable divine gift—would taste and see that You are good! Blessed is the woman who takes refuge in You! Be near to her when she is brokenhearted, saving her when she is crushed in spirit.

Say to her soul, "I am your salvation!" Then her soul will rejoice in You, exulting in Your salvation. May all her bones say, "O LORD, who is like You, delivering the poor from him who is too strong for him, the poor and needy from him who robs him?"

You have seen, O LORD; be not silent! O Lord, be not far from her! Then her tongue shall tell of Your righteousness and of Your praise all the day long.

Make her feast on the abundance of Your house, and give her drink from the river of Your delights. For with You is the fountain of life; in Your light do we see light. O continue Your steadfast love toward her, and Your righteousness to the upright of heart! Let not the foot of arrogance come upon her, nor the hand of the wicked drive her away.

Please fill her with grace daily, that her life might be a fountain of sweet water. Amen (Psalm 34, 35, 36).

$\mathcal{O}$God who hears the prayers of Your children,

Only You can bring my wife to trust in You and do good; to dwell in the land and befriend faithfulness. Only Your Hand can turn her heart like a stream of water to delight herself in You so that You will give her the desires of her heart.

O beloved, listen to my entreaty: commit your way to the LORD; trust in Him, and He will act. He will bring forth your righteousness as the light, and your justice as the noonday.

Father, let her be still before You and wait patiently for You; not fretting herself over the one who prospers in his way, over the man who carries out evil devices. For her steps are established by You, when You delight in her way; though she fall, she will not be cast headlong, for You uphold her hand.

It is my humble plea that her soul would take hope in Your words through David: "I have been young, and now am old, yet I have not seen the righteous forsaken or her children begging for bread."

May her mouth utter wisdom, and her tongue speak justice. May the law of her God be in her heart so that her steps do not slip (Psalm 37).

*Necessity!—I hardly like to talk of that, let me rather speak of the deliciousness of prayer—the wondrous sweetness and divine felicity which come to the soul that lives in the atmosphere of prayer. John Fox said, "The time we spend with God in secret is the sweetest time, and the best improved. Therefore, if thou lovest thy life, be in love with prayer." The devout Mr. Hervey resolved on the bed of sickness—"If God shall spare my life, I will read less and pray more." John Cooke, of Maidenhead, wrote—"The business, the pleasure, the honour, and advantage of prayer press on my spirit with increasing force every day." A deceased pastor when drawing near his end, exclaimed, "I wish I had prayed more"; that wish many of us might utter.*
~Charles Spurgeon

$\mathcal{L}$ORD of the cloud and fire,

The salvation of my wife is from You; You are her stronghold in the time of trouble. You help her and deliver her; please deliver her from the wicked and save her, because she takes refuge in You.

Do not forsake her, O LORD! O my God, be not far from her! Make haste to help her, O Lord, my salvation!

O LORD, make her know her end and what is the measure of her days; let her know how fleeting she is! Behold, You have made her days a few handbreadths, and her lifetime is as nothing before You. Surely all mankind stands as a mere breath!

Hear my prayer—may she wait patiently for You; incline to her and hear her cry. Draw her up from the pit of destruction, out of the miry bog, and set her feet upon a rock, making her steps secure. Put a new song in her mouth, a song of praise to her God. May many see her and fear, and put their trust in You.

Blessed is the woman who makes the LORD her trust. As for You, O LORD, do not restrain Your mercy from her; Your steadfast love and Your faithfulness will ever preserve her!

O beloved, hope in God! Amen (Psalm 37, 39, 40).

$\mathcal{O}$God most high, most glorious,

Be pleased to deliver her! O LORD, make haste to help her! Let those be put to shame and disappointed altogether who seek to snatch away her life.

But may she seek You and rejoice and be glad in You; may she love Your salvation and say continually, "Great is the LORD!" You are her help and her deliverer; do not delay, O my God! As the deer pants for flowing streams, so may her soul pant for You. May her soul thirst for God, for the living God.

When her soul is cast down and in turmoil within her, let her hope in You and praise You—her salvation and her God. By day You command Your steadfast love, and at night may Your song be with her, a prayer to the God of her life.

Send out Your light and Your truth; let them lead her; let them bring her to Your dwelling! Then take her to Your altar; let her delight in You as her exceeding joy and praise You with the lyre, O God, my God.

Why are you cast down, O my beloved, and why is your soul in turmoil within you? Hope in God; for He is worthy of praise, your salvation and your God! (Psalm 40, 42, 43).

*Only he who is himself secure and happy in the Lord can pray effectively for others.* ~Mike Mason

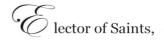 lector of Saints,

May my dear wife boast continually in You, and give thanks to Your Name forever.  Please redeem her for the sake of Your steadfast love!  Be her refuge and strength, a very present help in trouble.  Therefore we will not fear though the earth gives way, though the mountains be moved into the heart of the sea.

O God, be near her so that she will not be moved; help her when morning dawns.  Make her to be still and know that You are God.  And then let her clap her hands, shouting to You with loud songs of joy!

Know, my dearest, that the LORD, the Most High, is to be feared, a great king over all the earth.  Sing praises to God, sing praises!  Sing praises to our King, sing praises!  For God is the King of all the earth; sing praises with a psalm!

Cause her to think on Your steadfast love, O God.  Your praise reaches to the ends of the earth.  Your right hand is filled with righteousness.  Let her be glad!  Let this daughter of Judah rejoice because of Your judgments!

Ransom her soul from the power of Sheol, and out of her—the perfection of beauty—shine forth.

O beloved, shine forth the shimmering beauty of our Lord Christ!  Amen (Psalm 46, 47, 48, 49).

$\mathcal{O}$Living God,

Incline my wife's heart to offer You a sacrifice of thanksgiving. Have mercy on her according to Your steadfast love; according to Your abundant mercy blot out her transgressions. Wash her thoroughly from her iniquity, and cleanse her from her sin! Make her know her transgressions and in humility have her sin ever before her.

Purge her with hyssop, and she shall be clean; wash her, and she shall be whiter than snow. Let her hear joy and gladness; let the bones that You have broken rejoice. Hide Your face from her sins, and blot out all her iniquities. Create in her a clean heart, O God, and renew a right spirit within her.

Cast her not away from Your presence, and take not Your Holy Spirit from her. Most of all I pray, *restore unto her the joy of Your salvation*, and uphold her with a willing spirit. Then her tongue will sing aloud of Your righteousness. O Lord, open her lips, so that her mouth will declare Your praise.

O my gift of heaven, the sacrifices of God are a broken spirit; a broken and contrite heart He will not despise (Psalm 50 & 51).

*Why are we called "adulteresses" in praying for something to spend on our pleasures? Because God is our husband and the "world" is a prostitute luring us to give affections to her that belong only to God. This is how subtle the sin of worldliness can be. It can emerge not against prayer, but in prayer—and fasting. We begin to pray and fast—even intensely—not for God as our all-satisfying husband, but only for his gifts in the world so that we can make love with them.*
~John Piper

*H*oly LORD,

Make my treasured wife trust in Your steadfast love forever and ever. May she thank You forever, because You are saving her. O that she would wait for Your Name, for it is good.

Save her, by Your Name, and vindicate her by Your might. O God, hear my prayer; give ear to the words of my mouth. Hide not Yourself from my plea for mercy! Sustain her as she casts her burden upon You; when she is afraid let her trust in You.

In You, whose word we praise, in You we trust; we shall not be afraid. What can flesh do to us? This we know, that You are *for* us.

O beloved, do not be afraid, for what can man do to you? God is *for* you! You need not fear.

Deliver her soul from death, yes, her feet from falling, that she may walk before You in the light of life. Be merciful to her, O God, be merciful to her, for in You her soul takes refuge; in the shadow of Your wings let her take refuge, till the storms of destruction pass by.

Fulfill Your purpose for her and be exalted above the heavens. Let Your glory be over all the earth!

Dearest beloved, sing and make melody with me! We give thanks to You, O Lord, among the peoples; we will sing praises to You among the nations. For Your steadfast love is great to the heavens, Your faithfulness to the clouds (Psalm 52, 54, 56, 57).

$\mathcal{O}$Changeless God,

Deliver my priceless wife from her enemies; protect her from those who rise up against her. Then she shall sing of Your strength; make her sing aloud of Your steadfast love in the morning. For You have been to her a fortress and a refuge in the day of her distress. O my Strength, we will sing praises to You, for You, O God, are our fortress, the God who shows us steadfast love.

Hear my cry, listen to her prayer; from the end of the earth may she call to You when her heart is faint. Lead her to the rock that is higher than she, for You are a refuge, a strong tower against the enemy. Let her dwell in Your tent forever! Let her take refuge under the shelter of Your wings! Appoint steadfast love and faithfulness to watch over her!

May she wait for You alone in silence; from You comes salvation. You alone must be her rock and her salvation, her fortress; let her not be greatly shaken. Her hope must come from You.

Trust in Him at all times, my beloved; pour out your heart before Him; God is a refuge for us. Amen (Psalm 59, 61, 62).

$\mathcal{My}$ Father,

May my wonderful wife earnestly seek You; might her soul thirst for You; make her flesh faint for You, as in a dry and weary land where there is no water. Let her look upon You continually, beholding Your power and glory. And because she knows with every fiber of her being that Your steadfast love is better than life, may her lips praise You.

Form her into a woman who will bless You as long as she lives, lifting up her hands in Your Name. Satisfy her soul as with fat and rich food. And I ask that she remember You even upon her bed, and meditate on You in the watches of the night, her mouth praising You with joyful lips. For You have been her help, and in the shadow of Your wings she will sing for joy.

O beloved, let your soul cling to God, for His right hand upholds you! (Psalm 63).

*How, then, do you pray? Do you ask God for your daily bread? Do you thank God for your conversion? Do you pray for the conversion of others? If the answer is 'no', I can only say that I do not think you are yet born again. But if the answer is 'yes'—well, that proves that, whatever side you may have taken in debates on this question in the past, in your heart you believe in the sovereignty of God no less firmly than anyone else. On our feet we may have arguments about it, but on our knees we are all agreed.* ~J.I. Packer

$\mathcal{L}$ord and King,

Let my winsome wife rejoice in You and take refuge in You! Let her upright heart exult! Praise is due to You, O God—You who hear prayers. Blessed is the one You choose and bring near, to dwell in Your courts! Please secure her place among such chosen.

Shout for joy to God, my beloved; sing the glory of His Name; give to Him glorious praise! Say to God, "How awesome are Your deeds! So great is Your power that Your enemies come cringing to You. All the earth worships You and sings praises to You; they sing praises to Your Name."

May she rejoice in You, who rule by Your might forever. Test her and try her as silver is tried. Please, please do not reject her prayer or remove Your steadfast love from her! Instead be gracious to her and bless her and make Your face shine upon her, that Your way may be known on earth, Your saving power among all the nations. May she be glad, exulting before You, jubilant with joy! (Psalm 64, 66, 68).

$\mathcal{G}$od of Grace,

Make my wife sure of this: that You who began a good work in her will bring it to completion at the day of Christ Jesus. For You alone are my witness, how I yearn for her with the affection of Christ Jesus, and when I do not, assist me to yearn for her as I ought. It is my prayer that her love may abound more and more, with knowledge and all discernment, so that she may approve what is excellent, and so be pure and blameless for the day of Christ, filled with the fruit of righteousness that comes through Jesus Christ, to the glory and praise of Your name.

With special grace I ask that You would enable her to count whatever gain she has as loss for the sake of Christ. Indeed, make her count everything as loss because of the surpassing worth of knowing Christ Jesus her Lord. May she suffer along with me the loss of all things and count them as rubbish, in order that she may gain Christ and be found in Him, not having a righteousness of her own that comes from the law, but that which comes through faith in Christ, the righteousness from You that depends on faith—that she may *know* Christ and the power of His resurrection, and may share in His sufferings, becoming like Him in His death (Philippians 1 & 3).

*A*mighty God,

Be to my dear wife a rock of refuge, to which she may continually come. For You, O Lord, are her hope.

May her mouth be filled with Your praise, and with Your glory all the day. O God, be not far from her; O my God, make haste to help her! May she hope continually and praise You yet more and more. Let her mouth tell of Your righteous acts, of Your deeds of salvation all the day, for their number is past knowledge.

So even to old age and gray hairs, O God, do not forsake her, until she proclaims Your might to another generation, Your power to all those to come (Psalm 71).

*Among all the formative influences which go to make up a man honoured of God in the ministry, I know of none more mighty than his own familiarity with the mercy-seat. All that a college course can do for a student is coarse and external compared with the spiritual and delicate refinement obtained by communion with God. While the unformed minister is revolving upon the wheel of preparation, prayer is the tool of the great potter by which he moulds the vessel. All our libraries and studies are mere emptiness compared with our closets. We grow, we wax mighty, we prevail in private prayer.*
~Charles Spurgeon

$\mathcal{B}$lessed be the LORD, the God of Israel, who alone does wondrous things.

Blessed be Your glorious Name forever; may the whole earth be filled with Your glory!

I come before You with this petition: that my exquisite wife would be continually with You—may You hold her right hand. Guide her with Your counsel, for it is perfect, wise, and good.

Cause these miraculous, marvelous words to pour from her soul: "Whom have I in heaven but You? And there is nothing on earth that I desire besides You." I know that her heart and her flesh may fail, therefore be the strength of her heart and her portion forever.

As for my wife, it is good for her to be near You; let her make You her refuge, that she may tell of all Your works. Continue to mold her into a woman who fears You, for who can stand before You once Your anger is roused?

O beloved, remember the deeds of the LORD; yes, remember His wonders of old. Ponder all His work, and meditate on His mighty deeds.

Your way, O God, is holy. What god is great like our God? You are the God who works wonders; You have made known Your might among the peoples. O please work wonders on her behalf, and with Your arm redeem her (Psalm 72, 73, 76, 77).

$\mathcal{G}$od of peace,

It is my request that my wife would set her hope in You and not forget Your works, but keep Your commandments. Let her not be like this stubborn and rebellious generation, a generation whose heart is not steadfast, whose spirit is not faithful to You. Make her heart steadfast toward You and faithful to Your covenant. Thank You for being compassionate, atoning for her iniquity, and not destroying her; You restrained Your anger from her and did not stir up all Your wrath.

Remember that she is but flesh, a wind that passes and comes not again. Restore her, O God of hosts; let Your face shine, that she may be saved!

O beloved, call to Him who alone is your salvation! With all your might seek His wonderful, matchless face! (Psalm 78 & 80).

*God has designed not only that prayer come to be, but that prayer sometimes be a necessary means for accomplishing the ends he has ordained. In other words, God purposely designed how things would work so that some of what he accomplishes can only be accomplished as people pray. ~Bruce Ware*

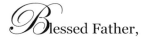**lessed Father,**

My wife needs to need You. O that her soul would long, yes, faint for Your courts; that her heart and flesh would sing for joy to You, the living God. Give her a thankful heart, ever singing Your praise! Bless her with a grateful soul, exalting Your Name forever.

O treasured wife, sing aloud to God your strength; shout for joy to the God of Jacob! Raise a song; sound the tambourine, the sweet lyre with the harp.

LORD God of hosts, hear my prayer; give ear, O God of Jacob! Bring her into Your presence, for a day in Your courts is better than a thousand elsewhere. May she rather be a doorkeeper in Your house than dwell in the tents of wickedness.

Be her sun and her shield; bestow on her favor and honor. Withhold no good thing from her, because she walks uprightly. O LORD of hosts, blessed is the one who trusts in You! (Psalm 84).

$\mathcal{O}$Thou Giving God,

Be gracious to my wonderful wife, for to You do I cry all the day. Gladden the soul of Your servant, for to You, O Lord, do I lift up her soul.

Teach her Your way that she may walk in Your truth; unite her heart to fear Your Name. Turn to her and be gracious to her; give her strength, and save her.

O beloved, sing with me of the steadfast love of the LORD forever; with your mouth make known His faithfulness to all generations!

Make her walk in the light of Your face, exulting in Your Name all the day, exalted in Your righteousness. Teach her to number her days that she may get a heart of wisdom. Satisfy her in the morning with Your steadfast love, that she may rejoice and be glad all her days. Make her glad for the days You have afflicted her, and for as many years as she has seen evil. Let Your work be shown to her, and Your glorious power to her children. Amen (Psalm 86 & 89).

orious God,

Let Your favor be upon my sweetest of wives. Establish the work of her hands.

Be her dwelling place, Most High, and be her refuge, so that no evil shall be allowed to befall her. Command Your angels concerning her to guard her in all her ways. Because You hold fast to her in love, please deliver her; protect her because she knows Your Name.

When she calls to You, answer her; be with her in trouble; rescue her and honor her. With long life satisfy her, and show her Your salvation. Satisfy her with Your beauty.

Hear, my beloved, while I admonish you! Listen to me: there shall be no strange god before you; you shall not bow down to a foreign god. Go to the LORD! Open your mouth wide, and He will fill it. He will feed you with the finest of wheat, and with honey from the rock He will satisfy you (Psalm 90, 91, 81).

*Prayer is the process of crouching down and making ourselves small before God. This downsizing is not an option; it is the only way to enter the kingdom of heaven. To grow in the Spirit is to become little in relation to more and more areas of life—marriage, family, church, work—until eventually it is possible to be little and childlike even in the presence of Satan and all his demons. For it is God, not you or I, who is bigger than evil.* ~Mike Mason

$\mathcal{F}$aithful Creator,

May grace and peace be multiplied to my matchless wife in the knowledge of You and of Jesus our Lord. May she grow in the grace and knowledge of our Lord and Savior Jesus Christ. When she suffers according to Your will, let her entrust her soul to a faithful Creator while doing good.

Let her not love the world or the things in the world, and may she keep herself from idols.

O beloved, do not love what is passing away more than your God! Instead build yourself up in your most holy faith; pray in the Holy Spirit; keep yourself in the love of God, waiting for the mercy of our Lord Jesus Christ that leads to eternal life.

Now to Him who is able to keep you from stumbling and to present you blameless before the presence of His glory with great joy, to the only God, our Savior, through Jesus Christ our Lord, be glory, majesty, dominion, and authority, before all time and now and forever. Amen (II Peter 3, I John 2, Jude).

*G*lorious and Holy God,

You have made me glad by Your work; at the works of Your hands I sing for joy. How great are Your works, O LORD, for You have made my beautiful wife! Your thoughts are very deep! Therefore keep her in Your care, and discipline her, and teach her out of Your law. For blessed is the woman whom You discipline, to give her rest from days of trouble. Do not forsake her or abandon her as Your heritage.

If You are not her help, her soul would soon live in the land of silence. When her foot slips, hold her up, O LORD, with Your steadfast love. When the cares of her heart are many, cheer her soul with Your consolations. Become her stronghold, and her rock of refuge.

Oh come, my beloved, and let us sing to the LORD; let us make a joyful noise to the rock of our salvation! Let us come into His presence with thanksgiving; let us make a joyful noise to Him with songs of praise! For You, O LORD, are a great God, and a great King above all gods (Psalm 92, 94, 95).

*If we do not learn to pray, it will not be for want of instructions and examples. Look at Abraham, taking it upon him to speak unto the Lord for Sodom. Look at Isaac, who goes out to meditate in the field at the eventide. Look at Jacob, as he wrestles until the breaking of the day at the Jabbok. Look at Hannah, as she speaks in her heart. Look at David, as he prevents now the dawning of the day, and now the watches of the night, in a hundred psalms. Look at our Lord. And then, look at Paul, as great in prayer as he is in preaching, or in writing Epistles. No, –if you never learn to pray, it will not be for want of the clearest instructions, and the most shining examples.* ~Alexander Whyte

$\mathcal{L}$ord Christ,

Only by Your blood and imputed righteousness do I approach the Father with confidence concerning my priceless wife.

Therefore, Father, as she received Christ Jesus the Lord, may she so walk in Him, rooted and built up in Him and established in the faith, just as she was taught, abounding in thanksgiving.

O beloved, if then you have been raised with Christ, seek the things that are above, where Christ is, seated at the right hand of God. Set your mind on things that are above, not on things that are on earth. For you have died, and your life is hidden with Christ in God.

Father, help her to walk in her new self, which is being renewed in knowledge after the image of its creator. Assist her to put to death what is earthly in her: sexual immorality, impurity, passion, evil desire, and covetousness, which is idolatry. Let her put them all away: anger, wrath, malice, slander, and obscene talk from her mouth. You are the great healer and refiner. Purify my wonderful wife by whatever means are necessary. Make her wholly Yours. Amen (Colossians 2 & 3).

 ORD God Almighty,

Grant that my wife declare Your glory among the nations; Your marvelous works among all the peoples. For great are You LORD, and greatly to be praised; You are to be feared above all gods. Splendor and majesty are before You; strength and beauty are in Your sanctuary.

May my wife ascribe to You glory and strength! Let her ascribe to You the glory due Your Name, worshiping You in the splendor of holiness. Make her say among the nations, "The LORD reigns!"

Let her hear of Your righteousness and be glad, rejoicing with the daughters of Judah because of Your judgments, O LORD. May she hate evil, for You preserve the lives of Your saints; You deliver them from the hand of the wicked.

O beloved come, let us worship and bow down; let us kneel before the LORD, our Maker! For He is our God, and we are the people of His pasture, and the sheep of His hand (Psalm 96 & 95).

*Resolved, never to count that a prayer, nor to let that pass as a prayer, nor that as a petition of a prayer, which is so made, that I cannot hope that God will answer it; nor that as a confession, which I cannot hope God will accept.*
~Jonathan Edwards

 ternal Father,

With Your right hand and Your holy arm please work salvation for my dearest wife. Remember Your steadfast love and faithfulness to Your daughter so that all the ends of the earth will see the salvation of her God.

Make a joyful noise to the LORD, my beloved; break forth into joyous song and sing praises! Join with the sea as it roars, with the world and those who dwell in it, with the rivers as they clap their hands, with the hills singing for joy together before the LORD.

O God, may she ponder the way that is blameless, and walk in integrity of heart. Let her not set before her eyes anything that is worthless, keeping a perverse heart far from her.

Do not hide Your face from her in the day of her distress! Incline Your ear to her; answer speedily when she calls! And by Your infinite mercy grant her heart to pour forth in song, "Bless the LORD, O my soul, and all that is within me, bless His holy Name" (Psalm 98, 102, 103).

*It is crucial that we not be more fascinated, more gripped, by the prayers of a man than by the pleasures of God. How easy it is to be more thrilled by radical devotion than by divine beauty.* ~John Piper

 less the LORD, O my soul!

O LORD my God, You are very great! You are clothed with splendor and majesty, covering Yourself with light as with a garment. And by the blood and mercy of Your perfect Son I appeal to Your wise power on behalf of my wife.

May her meditation be pleasing to You, for she rejoices in You. Let her thank You for Your steadfast love, for Your wondrous works to the children of men! Satisfy her longing soul; when her soul hungers fill it with good things. Send out Your word and heal her, and deliver her from destruction. Let her sing and make melody with all her being!

Awake, my beloved! Let us awake the dawn! Give thanks with me to the LORD among the peoples; we will sing praises to Him among the nations. For Your steadfast love, O God, is above the heavens; Your faithfulness reaches to the clouds. Be exalted, O God, above the heavens! Let Your glory be over my wife! Amen (Psalm 104, 107, 108).

LORD,

Grant my wife help against the foe, for vain is the salvation of man! With You she shall do valiantly. O GOD my Lord, deal on her behalf for Your Name's sake; because Your steadfast love is good, deliver her! With her mouth let her give great thanks to You, praising You in the midst of sorrow. For You stand at the right hand of the needy, to save her from those who condemn her soul to death.

Praise be to You, LORD! I will give thanks to You with my whole heart, in the company of the upright, in the congregation. Great are Your works, studied by all who delight in them. Therefore help me to study my wife diligently, for she is Your wonderful handiwork. Her beauty exalts You and proves true Your word, for she is full of splendor and majesty.

Show her the power of Your works—that they are faithful and just; all Your precepts are trustworthy; they are established forever and ever, to be performed with faithfulness and uprightness.

O beloved, fear the LORD, for it is the beginning of wisdom; all those who practice this fear have a good understanding. His praise endures forever! (Psalm 108, 109, 111).

$\mathcal{O}$Divine Comforter,

When my dear wife sows in tears, let her reap with shouts of joy. Grant her assurance in the God of her salvation, hoping in You and Your steadfast love.

May she wait for You, and hope in Your word. Continually make her into a woman whose soul waits for You more than watchmen for the morning.

O beloved, hope in the LORD! For with the LORD there is steadfast love, and with Him is plentiful redemption. Hope in the LORD from this time forth and forevermore.

Lord God, make her like a fruitful vine within my house, and bless her with children like olive shoots around our table. Your blessing be upon her! I bless her in the Name of the LORD!

I praise You, LORD, for You are good; I sing to Your Name for it is pleasant! For You have chosen my wife for Yourself; she is Your own possession. Do as You please with her; deal with her according to Your sovereign purpose. For I know that You are great, and that You are above all gods (Psalm 126, 130, 128, 135).

*True religion makes us want to spend time alone in meditation and prayer. We read that this was true for Isaac (Gen. 24:63). Even more important, we read in the Gospels that Christ too needed to be alone with His Father. Concealing deep feeling is difficult, and yet grace-filled feeling is often more silent and private than that which is counterfeit.* ~Jonathan Edwards

iving God,

Remember my wonderful wife even in her low estate, for Your steadfast love endures forever. Though she walks in the midst of trouble, preserve her life; stretch out Your hand against the wrath of her enemies and deliver her. Please fulfill Your purposes for her; Your steadfast love, O LORD, endures forever. Do not forsake the work of Your hands.

O LORD, search her and know her! Hem her in, behind and before, and lay Your hand upon her.

I praise You, for she is fearfully and wonderfully made. Wonderful are Your works; my soul knows it very well. Her frame was not hidden from You, when she was being made in secret, intricately woven in the depths of the earth. Your eyes saw her unformed substance; in Your book were written, every one of them, the days that were formed for her, when as yet there were none of them.

Therefore take confidence, my beloved! The Almighty LORD of heaven and earth will accomplish for you what is best as His daughter. Faint not; be not downcast but sleep in His gracious providence, for when you awake He is still with you (Psalm 138 & 139).

*I myself have seen this rare beauty on the face of a young woman at prayer, one who most likely had no idea that she was being seen by human eyes. Her countenance was incomparably more lovely than anything Hollywood's cosmetology is able to achieve. Indeed, divine grace working in a receptive soul does produce what St. Paul calls "God's work of art" (Eph 2:10).* ~Thomas Dubay

*A*uthor of Salvation,

Being affectionately desirous of my wonderful wife, make me ready to share with her not only the gospel of God but also my own self, because she has become very dear to me. Now may You and the Lord Jesus direct her way, and make her increase and abound in love for all, so that You may establish her heart blameless in holiness before Yourself at the coming of our Lord Jesus with all His saints.

To this end I also pray for her: that You may make her worthy of Your calling and may fulfill every resolve for good and every work of faith by Your power, so that the Name of our Lord Jesus may be glorified in her, and her in Him, according to Your grace and the grace of the Lord Jesus Christ.

I ought always to give thanks to You for her, because You chose her to be saved, through sanctification by the Spirit and belief in the truth.

O beloved, to this He called you through our gospel, so that you may obtain the glory of our Lord Jesus Christ. So then, wonderful gift of heaven, stand firm and hold to the traditions that you were taught by His word.

Now may the Lord Jesus Christ Himself, and You, Father, who loved her and gave her eternal comfort and good hope through grace, comfort her heart and establish it in every good work and word. Amen (I Thessalonians 3 & II Thessalonians 1 & 2).

$\mathcal{G}$od of hosts,

Restore my wife; let Your face shine, that she may be saved! Search her, O God, and know her heart! Try her and know her thoughts! And see if there be any grievous way in her, and lead her in the way everlasting!

Set a guard, O LORD, over her mouth; keep watch over the door of her lips! Do not let her heart incline to any evil, to busy herself with wicked deeds. Let a righteous word strike her—it is a kindness; let it rebuke her—it is oil for her head; let her head not refuse it.

May she cry out to You, O LORD and say, "You are my refuge, my portion in the land of the living." Attend to her cry, especially when she is brought very low.

Cause her to remember the days of old, meditate on all that You have done, and ponder the work of Your hands. Let her stretch out her hands to You when her soul thirsts for You like a parched land. Hide not Your face from her, lest she be like those who go down to the pit.

Let her hear in the morning of Your steadfast love, for in You she trusts. Make her know the way she should go, for to You I lift up her soul. Amen (Psalm 80, 141, 142, 143).

 adiant Redeemer,

Teach her to do Your will, for You are her God! Let Your good
Spirit lead her on level ground! For Your Name's sake, O LORD,
preserve her life! In Your righteousness bring her soul out of
trouble.

I confess that she and I deserve none of these mercies, but only
death and wrath. For what is man that You regard him, or the son
of man that You think of him? Man is like a breath; his days are
like a passing shadow. But praise be to You, Christ Jesus, for Your
righteous obedience and perfect atonement.

O beloved, do you know His greatness? He is great and greatly
to be praised, and His greatness is unsearchable. Extol Him as
Your God and King. Every day bless Him and praise His name
forever and ever.

Grant, Lord God, that she be a woman who meditates on the
glorious splendor of Your majesty and on Your wondrous works.
A woman who speaks of the might of Your awesome deeds, and
declares Your greatness. A woman who pours forth the fame of
Your abundant goodness and sings aloud of Your righteousness.
Amen (Psalm 143, 144, 145).

*The magnificence of God is the source and measure of the magnificence
of prayer. "Think magnificently of God."* ~Alexander Whyte

$\mathcal{K}$ing of Kings,

I appeal to Your testimony concerning Yourself: that You are gracious and merciful, slow to anger and abounding in steadfast love. You are good to all, and Your mercy is over all that You have made. Therefore, be eternally kind towards my dear wife. Keep her in the love of Christ, and let her give thanks to You and bless You always.

May she speak of the glory of Your kingdom and tell of Your power. Let her make known to the children of man Your mighty deeds, and the glorious splendor of Your kingdom. For Your kingdom is an everlasting kingdom, and Your dominion endures throughout all generations.

My sweet beloved, *know* this God! He is righteous in all His ways and kind in all His works. Trust this God, for He is near to all who call on Him, to all who call on Him in truth. Love this God, for He fulfills the desire of those who fear Him, and preserves all who love Him.

Let her mouth speak Your praise, O LORD, and let all flesh bless Your holy Name forever and ever (Psalm 145).

*In our Lord's prayer, he told us to pray, "Your kingdom come, your will be done, on earth as it is in heaven" (Matt. 6:10). This indicates that the perfect will of God precedes my praying and yours. We are not told to pray, "your will be formed," but "your will be done."* ~Bruce Ware

rince of Peace,

Let my winsome wife praise You as long as she lives; let her sing praises to her God while she has being. Let her be glad in her Maker, rejoicing in her King! Let her praise Your Name with dancing, making melody to You with her voice. Please take pleasure in her song and adorn her with salvation.

Let her exult in glory; let her sing for joy on her bed. Let Your high praises be in her throat and Your word in her hands. May she praise You in Your sanctuary; praise You in Your mighty heavens! Make her praise You for Your mighty deeds; praise You according to Your excellent greatness!

Put not your trust in princes, my beloved, in a son of man, in whom there is no salvation. But blessed is she whose help is the God of Jacob, whose hope is in the LORD her God, who made heaven and earth, the sea, and all that is in them, who keeps faith forever; who executes justice for the oppressed, who gives food to the hungry.

Everything that has breath praise the LORD! Praise the LORD! (Psalm 146, 149, 150).

# Wise Counselor,

I ask that my wife would hear Your instruction and not forsake Your teaching, for they are a graceful garland for her head and pendants for her neck. All good things come from You, O God, therefore make her ear attentive to wisdom and incline her heart to understanding; yes, let her call out for insight and raise her voice for understanding, seeking it like silver and searching for it as for hidden treasures. Give her such fervor so that she might understand the fear of You and find the knowledge of God.

Let not steadfast love and faithfulness forsake her; bind them around her neck; write them on the tablet of her heart.

Trust in the LORD with all your heart, my beloved! And lean not on your own understanding. In all your ways acknowledge Him, and He will make straight your paths. Be not wise in your own eyes; fear the LORD, and turn away from evil.

Lord God, may she honor You with her wealth and with the firstfruits of all her produce; then her barns will be filled with plenty, and her vats will be bursting with wine. Let her not despise Your discipline or be weary of Your reproof, for You reprove her whom You love, as a father the daughter in whom he delights.

Finally, I am wholly dependent on You to keep me as hers alone. Make me serve her with all fidelity, drinking water from my own cistern, flowing water from my own well. For why should my springs be scattered abroad, streams of water in the streets?

Keep her also faithful to me. Cause my fountain to be blessed, may I rejoice in the wife of my youth, a lovely deer, a graceful doe. Let her breasts fill me at all times with delight, that I may be intoxicated always in her love. Amen (Proverbs 1, 2, 3, 5).

*Better be somewhat too bold and somewhat unseemly than altogether to neglect and forget Almighty God. Better say that so bold saying, —"I will not let Thee go," than pray with such laziness and sleepiness and stupidity as we now pray.* ~Alexander Whyte

$\mathcal{F}$ather of our Lord Jesus,

May You direct the heart of my wife to Your love and to the steadfastness of Christ. Work this miracle of grace in her: that she would count it all joy when she meets trials of various kinds.

If she lacks wisdom, let her ask You, who give generously to all without reproach, so that it will be given her. Cause her to be a doer of the word, and not a hearer only, deceiving herself.

Though she has not seen You, let her love You. Though she does not now see You, let her believe in You and rejoice with joy that is inexpressible and filled with glory, obtaining the outcome of her faith, the salvation of her soul.

O beloved, it is my greatest joy and privilege to remind you that you are of a chosen race, a royal priesthood, a holy nation, a people for God's own possession, that you may proclaim the excellencies of Him who called you out of darkness into His marvelous light. O remember! Once you were an orphan, but now you are God's child; once you had not received mercy, but now you have received mercy!

To You alone, Lord God, be glory forever! Amen (James 1 & I Peter 1 & 2).

$\mathcal{G}$od of Truth,

Please be my lovely wife's confidence, and keep her foot from being caught. May she keep hold of instruction and not let it go; let her guard it, for it is her life. Make her commit her work to You so that her plans may be established.

O beloved, better is a little with the fear of the LORD than great treasure and trouble with it. The fear of the LORD is a fountain of life, that you may turn away from the snares of death.

Father, importunately I ask that she would find wisdom and get understanding, for the gain from it is better than gain from silver and its profit better than gold. May she consider wisdom as more precious than jewels, for long life is in her right hand; in her left hand are riches and honor. Let her not lose sight of these— sound wisdom and discretion, for they will be life for her soul and adornment for her neck (Proverbs 3, 16, 15).

*There is no true prayer without agony. Perhaps this is the problem in many of our churches. What little prayer we have is shallow, timid, carefully censored, and full of oratorical flourishes and hot air. There is little agony in it, and therefore little honesty or humility. We seem to think that the Lord is like everyone else we know, and that He cannot handle real honesty. So we put on our Sunday best to visit Him, and when we return home and take off our fancy duds we are left alone with what is underneath: the dirty underwear of hypocrisy.* ~Mike Mason

_M_aker of Life,

An excellent wife who can find?  O, but I have found one—or more truly, You have given one to me.  She is far more precious than jewels.  My heart trusts her, and I will have no lack of gain. She does me good, and not harm.  Thank You that she works with willing hands.  Thank You that she rises while it is yet night and provides food for her household.  Only by Your grace does she dress herself with strength and make her arms strong.  I praise You that she opens her hand to the poor and reaches out her hands to the needy.

She opens her mouth with wisdom, and the teaching of kindness is on her tongue; for this gratitude is due Your name. Thank You that she looks well to the ways of her household and does not eat the bread of idleness.  May my children rise up and call her blessed.

O beloved, many women have done excellently, but by grace you surpass them all!  You fear the LORD, therefore I will praise Him for you!  Praise the LORD all the earth!  Sing the glory of His Name; give to Him glorious praise!  Let everything that has breath praise the LORD, for He commanded, and my wife—my greatest and most beautiful earthly good—was created! (Proverbs 31 & Psalm 150).

$\mathscr{L}$ord and Father,

Thank You for calling my dear wife to belong to Jesus Christ. I praise You for loving her and calling her to be among the saints!

Grant that we may be mutually encouraged by each other's faith. And let her never be ashamed of the gospel, for it is the power of God for salvation to everyone who believes. For in it Your righteousness is revealed from faith for faith.

Indeed, when she was outside of Christ she failed to please You; she could not. She was not righteous, and there was no fear of You before her eyes.

O beloved, remember your depravity—the low estate from which He saved you! You have sinned and fallen short of His glory, and are justified by His grace as a gift, through the redemption that is in Christ Jesus, whom God put forward as a propitiation by His blood. And this was to show His righteousness, so that He might be just and the justifier of the one who has faith in Jesus.

Therefore she cannot boast, O LORD, for all that she has is of grace through Christ! May she live and breathe and eat and drink by grace alone, for Your glory alone (Romans 1 & 3).

*God has made the spread of his fame hang on the preaching of his Word; and he has made the preaching of his Word hang on the prayers of the saints. This is the awesome place of prayer in the purposes of God for the world. The triumph of the Word will not come without prayer.* ~John Piper

*H*oly Father,

Your servant David exults by saying, "Blessed are those whose lawless deeds are forgiven, and whose sins are covered." Therefore, please do not count the sin of my dear wife against her! I know that there will be tribulation and distress for every human being who does evil, and my wife has been wicked, as have I. We have had hard and impenitent hearts, thus storing up wrath for ourselves on the day of wrath when Your righteous judgment will be revealed. We have dishonored You by breaking Your wonderful law. Your name has been blasphemed among the Gentiles because of us. But thank You that for Your namesake You impute to my wife the righteousness of Your Son. By Your Holy Spirit keep her trusting in Christ's perfection alone, for You raised Him from the dead for our justification after He had been delivered up for our trespasses.

Therefore, my beloved, since you have been justified by faith, you have peace with God through our Lord Jesus Christ! O embrace and kiss Him! For through Him you have also obtained access by faith into this grace in which you stand. Let us, therefore, together rejoice in hope of the glory of God.

More than that, Father, help us to rejoice in our sufferings, knowing that suffering produces endurance, and endurance produces character, and character produces hope, and hope does not put us to shame, because Your love has been poured into our hearts through the Holy Spirit who has been given to us. Amen

(Romans 2 & 5).

*I*ncomparable God,

I praise You that while my wife was still weak and ungodly, Christ died for her. For one will scarcely die for a righteous person, but You have shown Your love for her in that while she was still a sinner, Christ died for her.

O beloved, since therefore you have been justified by His blood, much more shall you be saved by Him from the wrath of God. Rejoice! Rejoice in God through our Lord Jesus Christ, through whom you have now received reconciliation.

Father, let her not continue in sin so that grace may abound. May it never be! Do not allow her to live in sin once she has died to it. Cause her to consider herself dead to sin and alive to You in Christ Jesus. Let not sin reign in her mortal body, to make her obey its passions. Keep her from presenting her members to sin as instruments for unrighteousness. For sin will have no dominion over her, since she is not under law but under grace.

Just as she once presented her members as slaves to impurity and to lawlessness leading to more lawlessness, so now may she present her members as slaves to righteousness leading to sanctification. Instill this truth ever deeply within her: the wages of sin is death, but Your free gift is eternal life in Christ Jesus our Lord. Restrain her from earning deadly wages. And come quickly, Lord Jesus. We long for You. Amen (Romans 5 & 6).

$\mathcal{D}$eliciously Gracious Master,

When my wife finds herself divided in her desires, help her. There will be times when she delights in Your law in her inner being, but she sees in her members another law waging war against the law of her mind and making her captive to the law of sin that dwells in her members. And when she cries, "Wretched woman that I am! Who will deliver me from this body of death?" make her hope in You through Jesus Christ her Lord!

O beloved, it is my joy to remind you that there is therefore now no condemnation for those who are in Christ Jesus. For the law of the Spirit of life has set you free in Christ Jesus from the law of sin and death.

O God, cause her to exult in the knowledge that You have done what the law, weakened by the flesh, could not do. By sending Your own Son in the likeness of sinful flesh and for sin, You condemned sin in the flesh, in order that the righteous requirement of the law might be fulfilled in us who walk not according to the flesh but according to the Spirit. Although her body is dead because of sin, give her life by the Spirit because of righteousness! Amen (Romans 7 & 8).

*Pray often, for prayer is a shield to the soul,*
*a sacrifice to God, and a scourge for Satan.* ~John Bunyan

*A*bba, Father,

I ask on behalf of my darling wife, that Your Spirit would bear witness with her spirit that she is Your child. For she did not receive a spirit of slavery to fall back into fear, but You granted her the Spirit of adoption as a daughter. Cause her to live according to Your Spirit and not according to the flesh. For if she lives according to the flesh she will die, but if by the Spirit she puts to death the deeds of the body she will live.

Please be faithful to bear witness with her spirit that she is Your child, and if a child, then an heir—Your heir and fellow heir with Christ, provided she suffer with Him in order that she may also be glorified with Him.

Therefore grant her the grace of strength to consider that the sufferings of this present time are not worth comparing with the glory that is to be revealed to her.

O beloved, be not discouraged when you groan inwardly as we wait eagerly for adoption as sons, the redemption of our bodies. For in this hope we were saved. Wait for it with patience.

O LORD, we long for the return of Your beautiful Son. Come quickly, Christ Jesus. Amen (Romans 8).

eloved God,

By Your Spirit, help my precious wife in her weakness. For she does not know what to pray for as she ought, therefore may Your Spirit be faithful to intercede for her with groanings too deep for words. For You, who search hearts, know what is the mind of the Spirit, because the Spirit intercedes for the saints according to Your will.

O my beautiful wife, know for certain that for those who love God all things work together for good, for those who are called according to His purpose. For those whom He foreknew he also predestined to be conformed to the image of His Son, in order that He might be the firstborn among many brothers.

Father, thank You for Your sovereign choice; for loving her into faith in Christ, for predestining her to be conformed to His blessed image! Be magnified and lifted high for Your perfect work in her. Amen (Romans 8).

*There is a general kind of praying which fails for lack of precision.*
*It is as if a regiment of soldiers should all fire off their guns anywhere.*
*Possibly somebody would be killed, but the majority of the enemy would*
*be missed.* ~Charles Spurgeon

*A*mighty Infinite Father,

If You are for my beloved wife, who can be against her? You who did not spare Your own Son but gave Him up for us all, how will You not also with Him graciously give her all things? Who shall bring any charge against her as Your elect? It is You who justify. Who is to condemn? Assure her with the truth that Christ Jesus is the one who died—more than that, who was raised—who is at Your right hand, who indeed is interceding for her. I praise You that no one shall separate her from the love of Christ. Even tribulation, or distress, or persecution, or famine, or nakedness, or danger, or sword shall not prevail over His love.

Do you trust His grasp, my beloved? Do you hope in the triumph of God alone, even when you are killed all the day long and regarded as a sheep to be slaughtered? For in all these things we are more than conquerors through Him who loved us. You can be sure that neither death nor life, nor angels nor rulers, nor things present nor things to come, nor powers, nor height nor depth, nor anything else in all creation, will be able to separate us from the love of God in Christ Jesus our Lord (Romans 8).

*I have been driven many times to my knees by the overwhelming conviction that I had absolutely no other place to go.*
*~ Abraham Lincoln*

 ffectual Lover,

Your purpose of election must stand, for it is beautiful and wise to choose a people not because of works but because of Your call. May my dear wife learn to rejoice and tremble at Your words, "Jacob I loved, but Esau I hated." Let her not charge You with injustice because You are free. For You say to Moses, "I will have mercy on whom I have mercy, and I will have compassion on whom I have compassion." So then make her exult that it depends not on human will or exertion, but on You, who have mercy.

Let her love and fear the truth that You have mercy on whomever You will, and You harden whomever You will. Keep her from being a woman who questions You with arrogance, or sets her ways of justice above You, or demands You to account for what she finds inequitable. May she not question her molder, saying, "Why have You made me like this?" For You are the Lord and potter, and to You belongs the right to make one vessel for honored use and another for dishonorable use.

O beloved, my sweetest vessel of mercy, come, let us adore His goodness! In order to make known to us the riches of His glory He endured with much patience vessels of wrath prepared for destruction, to show His wrath and to make known His power.

Father, may Your Son be her greatest good forever. Amen (Romans 9).

*G*reat Shepherd of Your sheep,

My heart's desire and prayer is that my wife may be saved. Let her never be a woman who has a zeal for God, but not according to knowledge. Keep her from being ignorant of the righteousness that comes from You, and seeking to establish her own, thus failing to submit to Your righteousness. For Your Son is the end of the law for righteousness to everyone who believes.

Let this assurance ring afresh in her heart: that if she confesses with her mouth that Jesus is Lord and believes in her heart that You raised Him from the dead, she will be saved.

O beloved, adore the free goodness of our Lord's salvation! For the Scripture says, "Everyone who believes in Him will not be put to shame." For there is no distinction between Jew and Greek; the same Lord is Lord of all, bestowing His riches on all who call on Him. For "everyone who calls on the name of the Lord will be saved."

Father, You have told us that faith comes through hearing, and hearing through the word of Christ. Therefore use my wife to proclaim the good news so that her feet might be called beautiful. Amen (Romans 10).

$\mathcal{W}$ise Husbandman,

Thank You for choosing my wife by grace. And if it is by grace, it is no longer on the basis of works; otherwise grace would no longer be grace. Thank You for sparing her from hardening, from a spirit of stupor, from eyes that cannot see and ears that cannot hear.

Make her humbly grateful that some of the natural branches were broken off, and she, although a wild olive shoot, was grafted in among the others and now shares in the nourishing root of the olive tree. Let her never be arrogant toward the branches, remembering that it is not she who supports the root, but the root that supports her. Do not allow her to become proud, but cause her to stand in awe. For if You did not spare the natural branches, neither will You spare her.

My beloved, note then the kindness and the severity of God: severity toward those who have fallen, but God's kindness to you, provided you continue in His kindness. Otherwise you too will be cut off.

LORD God, lest we be wise in our own conceits, help us to understand this mystery: a partial hardening has come upon Israel, until the fullness of the Gentiles has come in. May we tremble before Your sovereign hand that has consigned all to disobedience, that You may have mercy on all.

Oh, the depth of Your riches and wisdom and knowledge! How unsearchable are Your judgments and how inscrutable Your ways! For who has known Your mind, or who has been Your counselor?  Or who has given a gift to You that he might be repaid?  For from You and through You and to You are all things. To You be glory forever.  Amen (Romans 11).

*When thou prayest, rather let thy heart be without words,*
*than thy words without a heart.*  ~John Bunyan

$\mathcal{M}$agnificent God,

I appeal to You by Your mercies, to receive my lovely wife's body as a living sacrifice, holy and acceptable to You. And grant her the willingness to present her body in this way, as her spiritual worship. Let her not be conformed to this world, but transform her by the renewal of her mind, that by testing she may discern what is Your will, what is good and acceptable and perfect.

May she not think of herself more highly than she ought to think, but rather think with sober judgment, according to the measure of faith that You have assigned. Enable her to use her gifts according to the grace given her: if prophecy, in proportion to her faith; if service, in her serving; if she teaches, in her teaching; if she exhorts, in her exhortation; if she contributes, in generosity; if she leads, with zeal; if she does acts of mercy, with cheerfulness.

O beloved, let your love be genuine. Abhor what is evil; hold fast to what is good. Love with sisterly affection. Let us outdo one another in showing honor. Do not be slothful in zeal, be fervent in spirit, serve the Lord.

Lord God, only by Your sovereign grace will she be able to rejoice in hope, be patient in tribulation, and be constant in prayer. Assist us together as we strive to contribute to the needs of the saints and seek to show hospitality. Amen (Romans 12).

*A*wesome LORD,

Only by Your unmerited favor will my sweet wife grow in likeness to Christ Jesus. So I entreat Your mercy on her behalf to enable her to bless those who persecute her; to bless and not curse them. Let her rejoice with those who rejoice, weep with those who weep, and live in harmony with her heavenly family. May she not be haughty, but associate with the lowly, giving herself to humble tasks. Let her never be conceited, nor repay anyone evil for evil. Instead grant that she give thought to do what is honorable in the sight of all. If possible, so far as it depends on her, make her live peaceably with all.

O beloved wife, never avenge yourself, but leave it to the wrath of God, for it is written, "Vengeance is mine, I will repay, says the LORD." To the contrary, if your enemy is hungry, feed him; if he is thirsty, give him something to drink; for by so doing you will heap burning coals on his head.

Holy God, do not let her be overcome by evil, but assist her to overcome evil with good; to cast off the works of darkness and put on the armor of light. Let her walk properly as in the daytime, not in orgies and drunkenness, not in sexual immorality and sensuality, not in quarreling and jealousy. But cause her to put on the Lord Jesus Christ, and make no provision for the flesh, to gratify its desires.

Come, Lord Jesus. We yearn for the day of Your unveiled beauty. Amen (Romans 12 & 13).

$\mathcal{O}$Thou who art faithful when we are faithless,

Let my dear wife not live to herself. If she lives, may she live to You, and if she dies, may she die to You. So that whether she lives or whether she dies, she might be Yours. For to this end Christ died and lived again, that He might be Lord both of the dead and of the living.

O beloved, do not pass judgment on your sister, or despise your brother. For we will all stand before the judgment seat of God; for it is written, "As I live, says the Lord, every knee shall bow to me, and every tongue shall confess to God." So then we will both give an account of ourselves to God.

Therefore Father, let her not pass judgment on her brothers and sisters any longer, but rather decide never to put a stumbling block or hindrance in their way. Cause her to pursue what makes for peace and for mutual upbuilding.

Remind her of her obligation as a woman of strength to bear with the failings of the weak, and not to please herself.

I ask, for the sake of Your Name, that through endurance and through the encouragement of the Scriptures she might have hope. May You enable us to live in such harmony with others, in accord with Christ Jesus, that together we may with one voice glorify You, the God and Father of our Lord Jesus Christ (Romans 14 & 15).

**God of Hope,**

May You fill my lovely wife with all joy and peace in believing, so that by the power of the Holy Spirit she may abound in hope. Fill her also with goodness and with all knowledge, enabling her to instruct others.

I appeal to you, my beloved, by our Lord Jesus Christ and by the love of the Spirit, to strive with me in your prayers to God on my behalf, that I may be delivered from my propensity to wander from the narrow road, so that by God's will I may serve you with joy and be refreshed in your company.

I appeal to You, Lord God, to give my wife discernment and vigilance to watch out for those who cause divisions and create obstacles contrary to the doctrine that she has been taught; may she avoid them. Safeguard her from their smooth talk and flattery by which they deceive the hearts of the naïve. For her obedience is known to all, so that I rejoice over her, but I want her to be wise as to what is good and innocent as to what is evil. Now to You who are able to strengthen her according to the gospel and the preaching of Jesus Christ, according to Your command, to bring about the obedience of faith—to You, the only wise God, be glory forevermore through Jesus Christ! Amen (Romans 15 & 16).

*Pray, and let God worry.* ~Martin Luther

$\mathcal{C}$hrist Jesus,

I praise You that in these last days God has spoken to us by You, His Son, whom He appointed heir of all things, through whom also He created the world.

Father, may my precious wife take pleasure in beholding Your Son as the radiance of Your glory and the exact imprint of Your nature, as He upholds the universe by the word of His power. May she exalt Him as much superior to angels as the name He has inherited is more excellent than theirs.

O beloved, join with me in saying, "Your throne, Lord Christ, is forever and ever, the scepter of uprightness is the scepter of Your kingdom. You have loved righteousness and hated wickedness; therefore God, Your God, has anointed You with the oil of gladness beyond Your companions."

You, Lord, laid the foundation of the earth in the beginning, and the heavens are the work of Your hands; they will perish, but You remain; they will all wear out like a garment, like a robe You will roll them up, like a garment they will be changed. But You are the same, and Your years have no end.

Father, cause her to adore Your magnificent Son incessantly and abound in thanksgiving for every glimpse of His beauty.

We long to see Him face to face. Amen (Hebrews 1).

$\mathcal{G}$racious Father,

I bow through Christ in prayer for the good wife You have granted me. I have deserved death, but You have given me beauty. I have earned hell, but You have provided a helper suitable for me. And for this I offer praise to Your great Son.

May my wife, who shares in my heavenly calling, consider Jesus, the apostle and high priest of our confession, who was faithful to You who appointed Him, just as Moses also was faithful in all Your house. For Jesus has been counted worthy of more glory than Moses—as much more glory as the builder of a house has more honor than the house itself. Now Moses was faithful in all Your house as a servant to testify to the things that were to be spoken later, but Christ is faithful over Your house as a son.

O beloved, we are His house if indeed we hold fast our confidence and our boasting in our hope.

Therefore Father, today, if she hears Your voice, let her not harden her heart as in the rebellion. Take care of her, lest there be in her an evil, unbelieving heart, leading her to fall away from the living God.

Help us to exhort one another every day, as long as it is called "today," that neither of us may be hardened by the deceitfulness of sin. For we share in Christ, if indeed we hold our original confidence firm to the end. Enable us to endure steadfastly! Enable us so that we might gain Your glorious Son!

Amen, come quickly Lord Jesus (Hebrews 3).

$\mathcal{G}$od of the living word,

Only through Christ, the great high priest, who is better than angels and greater than Moses—only through Him do I intercede for my wife. So I pray that while the promise of entering Your rest still stands she would fear lest she should seem to have failed to reach it. May Your good news meet with faith in her as she hears it.

I praise You that there remains a Sabbath rest for Your people, for whoever has entered Your rest has also rested from her works as You did from Yours. As the Scriptures say, "And God rested on the seventh day from all His works."

Let my cherished wife therefore strive to enter that rest, so that she may not fall by the same sort of disobedience that overtook all those who left Egypt led by Moses. For Your word is living and active, sharper than any two-edged sword, piercing to the division of soul and of spirit, of joints and of marrow, and discerning the thoughts and intentions of the heart. And no creature is hidden from Your sight, but all are naked and exposed to Your eyes. And to You we must give an account.

O beloved, since we have a great high priest who has passed through the heavens, Jesus, the Son of God, let us hold fast our confession. For we do not have a high priest who is unable to sympathize with our weaknesses, but one who in every respect has been tempted as we are, yet without sin. Let us then with confidence draw near to the throne of grace, that we may receive mercy and find grace in our time of need (Hebrews 4).

$\mathcal{S}$plendid Saviour,

It is my joy to trust and exalt You as the perfect source of eternal salvation to all who obey You.

Father, through Your Son I ask that my wonderful wife would never become dull of hearing, but instead crave solid food, developing skill in the word of righteousness. For solid food is for the mature. Therefore, please train her powers of discernment by constant practice to distinguish good from evil.

My beloved, let us leave the elementary doctrine of Christ and go on to maturity, not laying again a foundation of repentance from dead works and of faith toward God. And this we will do if God permits.

Therefore, Father, please be willing! Please permit her to go on to maturity. Keep her, and may she never be one who is enlightened, tastes the heavenly gift, shares in the Holy Spirit, tastes of the goodness of Your word, and then falls away. May it never be! (Hebrews 5 & 6).

*I must secure more time for private devotions. I have been living far too public for me. The shortening of devotions starves the soul, it grows lean and faint. I have been keeping too late hours.*
~William Wilberforce

*G*od of boundless mercy,

May my dear wife live as land that has drunk the rain that often falls on it, and produces a crop useful to those for whose sake it is cultivated, so that she might receive a blessing from You. But have mercy on her lest she bear thorns and thistles, for such land is worthless and near to being cursed, and its end is to be burned.

Assure her of better things—things that belong to salvation. For You are not so unjust as to overlook her work and the love that she has shown for Your sake in serving the saints, as she still does. And I desire Your work in her, causing her to show the same earnestness to have the full assurance of hope until the end, so that she may not be sluggish, but an imitator of those who through faith and patience inherit the promises.

Convince her by the unchangeable character of Your purpose that she is an heiress of the promise made to Abraham, that she might have strong encouragement to hold fast to the hope set before her.

O beloved, flee for refuge to Christ! For God has sworn by Himself and we have this promise as a sure and steadfast anchor of the soul, a hope that enters into the inner place behind the curtain, where Jesus has gone as a forerunner on our behalf, having become a high priest forever after the order of Melchizedek.

Lord Jesus, we exalt You as our hope and high priest! Please do not tarry in Your return (Hebrews 6).

$\mathcal{O}$lofty Lover of broken men,

I come to You on behalf of my wife through Jesus, the guarantor of a better covenant. Instill within her the wondrous assurance that Christ holds His priesthood permanently, because He continues forever. Consequently, He is able to save to the uttermost those who draw near to You through Him, since He always lives to make intercession for them. May she entrust herself wholly to Him, for it is fitting that she should have such a high priest, holy, innocent, unstained, separated from sinners, and exalted above the heavens.

May she exalt Him, for He has no need, like other high priests, to offer sacrifices daily, first for His own sins and then for those of the people, since He did this once for all when he offered up Himself. For the law appoints men in their weakness as high priests, but the word of the oath, which came later than the law, appoints a Son who has been made perfect forever. Let her cling to Him all the more!

O beloved, be assured that you have a better husband than I in Christ! For I pray for you in weakness, mortality, and with a wicked heart, but He is holy and perfect, and always lives to make intercession for you.

Father, assist us to love the Son's appearing (Hebrews 7).

*There is not in the world a kind of life more sweet and delightful than that of a continual conversation with God.* ~Brother Lawrence

$\mathcal{O}$God, my wealth and my salvation,

Sink deep within my priceless wife the understanding that she has a perfect and powerful high priest, one who is seated at the right hand of the throne of the Majesty in heaven, a minister in the holy places in the true tent that You set up, not man. For Christ has obtained a ministry that is as much more excellent than the old as the covenant He mediates is better, since it is enacted on better promises. Cause her to trust Christ's sacrifice alone, who through the eternal Spirit offered Himself without blemish to You. By His blood purify her conscience from dead works to serve You.

Take heart, my beloved, for Christ, having been offered once to bear the sins of many, will appear a second time, not to deal with sin but to save those who are eagerly waiting for Him.

Father, grant her such eagerness, that she may look forward to the day when her glorified Saviour returns. May she exult in His sacrifice, offered once for all time for sins, after which He sat down at Your right hand, waiting for that time until His enemies should be made a footstool for His feet. O let her praise and prize Him! For by a single offering He has perfected for all time those who are being sanctified (Hebrews 8, 9, 10).

*Prayer is as much a tool of our sanctification, by God's grace, as it is a tool of ministering God's grace to others.* ~Bruce Ware

*F*earful Judge,

Since my adorable wife now has confidence to enter the holy places by the blood of Jesus, by the new and living way that He opened for her through the curtain, that is, through His flesh, and since she has a great high priest over Your house, let her draw near to You with a true heart in full assurance of faith, with her heart sprinkled clean from an evil conscience and her body washed with pure water. May she hold fast the confession of her hope without wavering, for You who promised are faithful.

O beloved, let us consider how to stir one another to love and good works, not neglecting our time together, as is the habit of some, but encouraging one another, and all the more as we see the Day drawing near.

Father, keep her from going on sinning deliberately after receiving the knowledge of the truth, for if she does there no longer remains a sacrifice for sins, but a fearful expectation of judgment, and a fury of fire that will consume the adversaries. Please, please prevent her from spurning Your Son, or profaning the blood of the covenant by which she was sanctified, or outraging the Spirit of grace! For I know that vengeance is Yours; You will repay. "The Lord will judge His people." Sustain her! For it is a fearful thing to fall into the hands of the living God (Hebrews 10).

$\mathscr{S}$elf-sufficient God,

Only by Your worthy Son do I come to petition transforming and supporting grace for my wife. Because in You are all things good infinitely, I ask that she would grow in kindness and sympathy. Make her a woman who has compassion on those in prison, and who joyfully accepts the plundering of her property, knowing that she has a better possession and an abiding one. Let her not throw away her confidence, which has a great reward. For she has need of endurance, so that when she has done Your will she may receive what is promised. I thank You that she is not of those who shrink back and are destroyed, but of those who have faith and preserve their souls.

Raise her up as a woman of faith, having the assurance of things hoped for, the conviction of things not seen. For without faith it is impossible to please You, for whoever would draw near to You must believe that You exist and that You reward those who seek You. Make her like Sarah, who by faith received power to conceive, even when she was past the age, since she considered You faithful to Your promise.

O beloved, even though men and women like Sarah were commended through their faith, they did not receive what was promised, since God had provided something better for us, that apart from us they should not be made perfect. And now we have the Lord Jesus Christ! Bless His name with me!

Father, we long to see Your matchless Son. Let us praise His name forever, to Your glory. Amen (Hebrews 10 & 11).

$\mathcal{D}$isciplining Father,

Assist my lovely wife to lay aside every weight, and sin which clings so closely, and let her run with endurance the race that is set before her, looking to Jesus, the founder and perfecter of her faith, who for the joy that was set before Him endured the cross, despising the shame, and is seated at the right hand of Your throne.

O beloved, consider Him who endured from sinners such hostility against Himself, so that you may not grow weary or fainthearted. In our struggle against sin we have not yet resisted to the point of shedding our blood.

Great Father, remind her of the exhortation that addresses her as a daughter: "My daughter, do not regard lightly the discipline of the Lord, nor be weary when reproved by Him. For the Lord disciplines the one He loves, and chastises every daughter whom He receives."

Assure her that it is for discipline that she has to endure—that You are treating her as a daughter. For if she is left without discipline, in which all have participated, then she is an illegitimate child and not a daughter. May she not begrudge Your correction, but respect You and be subject to You, understanding that You discipline her for her good, that she may share in Your holiness. When Your discipline seems painful rather than pleasant, make her confident that later it yields the peaceful fruit of righteousness to those who have been trained by it (Hebrews 12).

$\mathcal{G}$entle and fearful Healer,

I bow through the merit of my Lord Christ, asking that You would lift my wife's beautiful drooping hands and strengthen her weak knees, and make straight paths for her feet, so that what is lame may not be put out of joint but rather be healed.

Cause her to strive for peace with everyone, and for the holiness without which no one will see You. May it never be that she fail to obtain Your grace! Protect her from any "root of bitterness" that springs up, causes trouble, and defiles many. Look after and guard her ways, that she may not be sexually immoral or unholy like Esau, who sold his birthright for a single meal. Have mercy! For I know that afterward, when he desired to inherit the blessing, he was rejected, for he found no chance to repent, though he sought it with tears.

O beloved, take refuge in Jesus, the mediator of a new covenant. See that you do not refuse the warnings of His Father. Flee to Christ, and you need not fear.

Father, help us as we strive to offer to You acceptable worship, with reverence and awe. For You are a consuming fire. Amen (Hebrews 12).

*Satan trembles when he sees*
*The weakest saint upon his knees.*
~William Cowper

$\mathcal{F}$aithful Helper,

Under the supreme sacrifice of Your Son I come on behalf of my beautiful wife. Please form her into a woman who does not neglect to show hospitality to strangers, for thereby some have entertained angels unawares. May she remember those who are in prison, as though in prison with them, and those who are mistreated.

Let marriage be held in honor by us both, and keep our marriage bed undefiled, for You will judge the sexually immoral and adulterous. Maintain her life free from the love of money, and make her content with what she has, for You have said, "I will never leave you nor forsake you."

Therefore, my beloved, you can confidently say, "The Lord is my helper; I will not fear; what can man do to me?"

Father, remind her of her leaders, those who spoke to her Your word. May she consider the outcome of their way of life, and imitate their faith, for Jesus Christ is the same yesterday and today and forever. Guard her from being led away by diverse and strange teachings, for it is good for the heart to be strengthened by grace, not by the food of carnal wisdom, which has not benefited those devoted to it.

Hasten the day of Your Son's appearing, we pray. Amen (Hebrews 13).

*My* dazzling Delight,

Through Christ Jesus I ask that You would put a willingness in my wife's heart to bear the reproach Your Son endured. May she grow to love the world less and love You more; to love me less and love You more. For here we have no lasting city, but we seek the city that is to come. Through Christ then let her continually offer up a sacrifice of praise to You, that is, the fruit of lips that acknowledge His name. Let her not neglect to do good and to share what she has, for such sacrifices are pleasing to You.

Cause us to obey our leaders and submit to them, for they are keeping watch over our souls, as those who will have to give an account.

O my best beloved on earth, adore with me the God that gives you worth! He has made you ever precious in my eyes. Therefore, may the God of peace who brought again from the dead our Lord Jesus, the great shepherd of the sheep, by the blood of the eternal covenant, equip you with everything good that you may do His will, working in you that which is pleasing in His sight, through Jesus Christ, to whom be glory forever and ever. Amen (Hebrews 13).

*Yes, love her, love her, more than life;*
*O, love the woman called your wife.*
*Go love her as your earthly best.*
*Beyond this venture not. But, lest*
*Your love become a fool's facade,*
*Be sure to love her less than God.*
*~John Piper*

*My* Sovereign Joy,

By Your beautiful Son and in His words I pray for my delightful wife. May she be counted among the poor in spirit, for theirs is the kingdom of heaven. Make her of those who mourn, for they shall be comforted. Bless her with meekness so that she will inherit the earth. Create within her a hunger and thirst for righteousness, for such women shall be satisfied. Let her be merciful so that she may receive mercy. Give her a pure heart so that she might see You. Number her among the peacemakers, for they shall be called Your children. When she is persecuted for righteousness' sake, may she be heartened that she is blessed and that hers is the kingdom of heaven.

O beloved, let me humbly remind you that you are blessed when others revile you and persecute you and utter all kinds of evil against you falsely on Christ's account. Rejoice and be glad, for your reward is great in heaven, for so they persecuted the prophets who were before you.

LORD, please be ever at work in her, molding her to be like Your Son. Amen (Matthew 5).

$\mathcal{M}$y gracious Father,

Through Jesus I kneel and ask that You would make my priceless wife a brilliant light to the world. Let her light shine before others, so that they may see her good works and glorify You.

May she do Your commandments and teach them so that she will be called great in the kingdom of heaven. For unless her righteousness exceeds that of the scribes and Pharisees, she will never enter the kingdom of heaven. Keep her from becoming angry with her brother, from murdering him in her heart, and thus becoming liable to judgment. Keep her from looking at a man with lustful intent, from committing adultery with him in her heart. If her right eye causes her to sin, let her tear it out and throw it away. For I would rather her lose one of her members than have her whole body thrown into hell. Instill within her a healthy fear of eternal fire.

Grant her humble longsuffering so as not to resist the person who is evil. But if anyone slaps her on the right cheek, let her turn to him the other also. And if anyone would sue her and take her tunic, may she let him have her cloak as well. And if anyone forces her to go one mile, let her go with him two miles. Make her a woman who gives to the one who begs from her, and who does not refuse the one who would borrow from her (Matthew 5).

oving Shepherd,

Please listen to my prayer because of Your Son's righteousness. I ask that You would incline the heart of my sweet wife to obey His commands. May she love her enemies and pray for those who persecute her, so that she may be Your daughter. For You make Your sun rise on the evil and the good, and send rain on the just and on the unjust.

O dear gift of heaven, if you love those who love you, what reward do you have? Does not even the world do the same? You therefore must be perfect, as your heavenly Father is perfect.

Lord, by Your Spirit continually work Your perfection in her! Help her to abstain from practicing her righteousness before other people in order to be seen by them, for then she will have no reward from You.

When she gives to the needy, do not let her left hand know what her right hand is doing, so that her giving may be in secret. For then You who see in secret will reward her.

And when she prays, keep her from being like the hypocrites who love to be seen and heard by others. Instead, cause her to go into her room and shut the door and pray to You who see in secret. Then, for what You see in secret please reward her. Amen (Matthew 5 & 6).

$\mathcal{F}$aithful Father,

Through Your Son I ask that You would keep my gentle wife obeying His words. May she not lay up for herself treasures on earth, where moth and rust destroy and where thieves break in and steal, but make her lay up for herself treasures in heaven, where neither moth nor rust destroys and where thieves do not break in and steal. For where her treasure is, there her heart will be also. And I long for her heart to love You unswervingly as its Treasure. She cannot serve two masters; she cannot serve You and money. Therefore keep her always as Your joyful, loyal servant.

Let her not be anxious about her life, what she will eat or what she will drink, nor about her body, what she will put on. For life is more than food, and the body more than clothing. Turn her eyes to the birds of the air and remind her—they neither sow nor reap nor gather into barns, and yet You feed them. And she is of much more value than they! Remind her that she cannot add a single hour to her span of life by being anxious. Guard her from being anxious about clothing, for the lilies of the field neither toil nor spin, yet even Solomon in all his glory was not arrayed like one of them.

My sweet beloved, trust your Master, lest He say, "O you of little faith." For if He clothes the grass of the field, which today is alive and tomorrow is thrown into the oven, will He not much more clothe you? Therefore do not be anxious, saying, "What shall we eat?" or "What shall we drink?" or "What shall we wear?"

For everyone seeks after all these things, and your heavenly Father knows that you need them all. But seek first the kingdom of God and His righteousness, and all these things will be added to you.

Therefore, Father, may she not be anxious about tomorrow, for tomorrow will be anxious for itself. Sufficient for the day is its own trouble (Matthew 6).

*I would exhort those who have entertained a hope of their being true converts—and who since their supposed conversion have left off the duty of secret prayer, and ordinarily allow themselves in the omission of it—to throw away their hope. If you have left off calling upon God, it is time for you to leave off hoping and flattering yourselves with an imagination that you are the children of God. Probably it will be a very difficult thing for you to do this. It is hard for a man to let go a hope of heaven, on which he hath once allowed himself to lay hold, and which he hath retained for a considerable time. True conversion is a rare thing; but that men should be brought off from a false hope of conversion—after they are once settled and established in it, and have continued in it for some time—is much more rare.*
~Jonathan Edwards

*E*verlasting King,

I bow through Christ for the sake of the fine and delicate wife You have granted me. May she judge not, that she be not judged. For with the judgment she pronounces she will be judged, and with the measure she uses it will be measured to her. Guide her away from hypocrisy, to first take the log out of her own eye, so that then she will see clearly to take the speck out of her sister's eye.

Make her wise to avoid giving dogs what is holy, and to not throw her pearls before pigs, lest they trample them underfoot and turn to attack her.

Cause her to ask, so that it will be given to her; to seek, so that she will find; to knock, so that it will be opened to her. Thank You for Your promise that everyone who asks receives, and the one who seeks finds, and to the one who knocks it will be opened. Remind her that if she, who is evil, knows how to give good gifts to her children, how much more will her Father who is in heaven give good things to those who ask Him!

Whatever she wishes that others would do to her, help her do also to them, for this is the Law and the Prophets. May she enter by the narrow gate. For the gate is wide and the way is easy that leads to destruction, and those who enter by it are many. For the gate is narrow and the way is hard that leads to life, and those who find it are few. Keep her steadfast on the hard way! May she never stray from it! For Your namesake let her foot not slip. Amen (Matthew 7).

$\mathcal{R}$ighteous Father,

Please protect my wife from false prophets, who come in sheep's clothing but inwardly are ravenous wolves. Make her wise to recognize them by their fruits. Help her to discern the healthy tree by its good fruit, and the diseased tree by its bad fruit. May she not be a diseased tree, for every such tree is cut down and thrown into the fire. Therefore, help her to bear much good fruit.

Let the warning of Your Son safeguard and preserve her when He says, "Not everyone who says to me, 'Lord, Lord,' will enter the kingdom of heaven, but the one who does the will of my Father who is in heaven." May He not say to her, "I never knew you; depart from me, you worker of lawlessness." No! Instead, please let her hear the words, "Well done, good and faithful servant." Through Jesus and by Your wonderful Spirit I ask these things. Amen (Matthew 7 & 25).

*The Spirit has much to do with acceptable prayer, and His work in prayer is too much neglected. He enlightens the mind to see its wants, softens the heart to feel them, quickens our desires after suitable supplies, gives clear views of God's power, wisdom, and grace to relieve us, and stirs up that confidence in His truth which excludes all wavering. Prayer is, therefore, a wonderful thing. In every acceptable prayer the whole Trinity is concerned. ~J. Angell James*

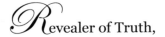**R**evealer of Truth,

Through Christ I ask that You would make my darling wife hear His words and do them, so that she may be like a wise man who built his house on a rock. Keep her from merely hearing His words and not doing them, for then she will be like the foolish man who built his house on the sand. When the rain falls, and the floods come, and the winds blow and beat against her, I do not wish her to fall! Your Word alone stands firm. May she build her life upon it.

Let her never despise or neglect tax collectors and sinners. But instead fill her with tenderness and compassion for them, and the humility to eat with them. For those who are well have no need of a physician, but those who are sick. Continue to teach her what this means: "I desire mercy, and not sacrifice." For Your great Son came not to call the righteous, but sinners (Matthew 7 & 9).

$\mathcal{M}$y Supreme and Everlasting Joy,

In this world my winsome wife is as a sheep in the midst of wolves, so please help her to be wise as a serpent and innocent as a dove. Prepare her for the persecution that lies along her pathway to heaven. Strengthen her to stand fast when men deliver her over to courts and flog her in their churches.

O beloved, when you are dragged before governors and kings for Christ's sake, do not be anxious how you are to speak or what you are to say, for what you are to say will be given to you in that hour. For it is not you who speak, but the Spirit of your Father speaking through you.

Lord God, make ready her heart for that dreadful time when brother will deliver brother over to death, and the father his child, and children will rise up against parents and have them put to death, and she will be hated by all for the sake of Christ's name. May she endure to the end and so be saved! Keep her! For Your hand is mightier than my own. Amen (Matthew 10).

*Prayer—secret, fervent, believing prayer—lies at the root of all personal godliness.* ~William Carey

electable God,

Grant my dear wife the grace to love Christ more than her father or mother, more than her son or daughter. For Your Son has said that if she fails to love Him supremely, she is not worthy of Him. And if she does not take her cross and follow Him, she is not worthy of Him. Therefore, because of Your grace and steadfast love, enable her to do so!

May she not find her life in this world and so lose it, but make her a woman who gladly loses her life for Jesus' sake so that she might find it.

Father, I know that it pleases You well to hide things from the wise and understanding and reveal them to little children. Therefore please grow her in childlikeness, show her Your matchless Son, and may He choose to reveal You increasingly to her.

O beloved of my heart, you who labor and are heavy laden, go to Christ, and He will give you rest. Take His yoke upon you, and learn from Him, for He is gentle and lowly in heart, and you will find rest for your soul.

Lord Christ, we praise and thank You that Your yoke is easy, and Your burden is light! Amen (Matthew 10 & 11).

*G*reat Covenant Keeper,

My wife cannot speak good if she is evil. For out of the abundance of the heart the mouth speaks. Therefore fill her with good treasure so that she might bring forth good. Make Christ her Treasure, so that she might speak His praise. For on the day of judgment she will give account for every careless word she speaks; so please do not let her be condemned by her words.

I praise You that to her it has been given to know the secrets of the kingdom of heaven, for to many it has not been given. Let her never be among those of whom it is said, "Seeing they do not see, and hearing they do not hear, nor do they understand." Keep her heart from growing dull. Help her to see with her eyes and hear with her ears and understand with her heart and turn, that You may heal her.

O beloved, your master Jesus has said that blessed are your eyes, for they see, and your ears, for they hear. Truly, I say to you, many prophets and righteous people longed to see what you see, and did not see it, and to hear what you hear, and did not hear it.

Father, it is You who have opened her eyes to behold the wonders of Your word and the glories of Your Son. Keep her vigilant. Amen (Matthew 12 & 13).

*No man can do me a truer kindness in this world*
*than to pray for me.* ~Charles Spurgeon

$\mathcal{S}$elf-exalting God,

May my precious wife never prove herself to be as one who, when she hears the word of the kingdom and does not understand it, the evil one comes and snatches away what has been sown in her heart. Guard her from the evil one! And let her not be like the one who hears the word and immediately receives it with joy, yet she has no root in herself, but endures for a while, and when tribulation or persecution arises on account of the word, immediately she falls away. Do not let her fall! Please grow her roots strong and deep in You.

Save her from being a woman who hears the word, but the cares of the world and the deceitfulness of riches choke the word, and it proves unfruitful. Instead, make her heart good soil, so that she hears the word and understands it, and bears fruit and yields a hundredfold (Matthew 13).

$\mathcal{S}$overeign Ruler and King,

Your Kingdom is like treasure hidden in a field, which a man found and covered up. Therefore, may my elegant wife be like that man, who, in his joy went and sold all that he had and bought the field.

Again, make her like the merchant in search of fine pearls, who, on finding one pearl of great value, went and sold all that he had and bought it. Let her count Christ her greatest treasure, her most valuable pearl, her ultimate source of joy. And may she stop at nothing to have Him.

Keep her from breaking Your commandments for the sake of tradition. May she never, for the sake of tradition, make void Your word. Indeed, unless You preserve her with grace she will be numbered among the hypocrites who honor You with their lips, but their heart is far from You; who worship You in vain, teaching as doctrines the commandments of men.

Let her take heart, and not be afraid, for it is You who keep her. Let her not doubt, for truly Jesus, the Son of God, is her righteousness (Matthew 13, 14, 15).

*No praying man or woman accomplishes so much with so little expenditure of time as when he or she is praying.* ~A.E. McAdam

$\mathcal{L}$ord of the heavens and the earth,

I come to You now petitioning more grace for my wonder-inspiring wife. Her heart needs continual cleansing, as does mine, because what proceeds from it is what defiles a person. For out of the heart come evil thoughts, murder, adultery, sexual immorality, theft, false witness, slander. These are what defile a person, therefore please create in her a clean heart.

O beloved, guard your heart. Watch and beware of the leaven of the Pharisees and Sadducees, of the sophistry of this age, of the false teachers who speak sweetly and humbly. Blessed are you if you know the truth of Christ. For flesh and blood has not revealed Him to you, but your Father who is in heaven.

O God, may she set her mind on the things of You, and not on the things of man. All this I ask in the name of the Christ, the Son of the living God. Amen (Matthew 15 & 16).

*M*y Mighty Fortress,

Thank You for giving me a magnificent wife who follows Your Son so faithfully. Assist her to continue going after Him, to deny herself and take up her cross and follow Him. May she not strive to save her life and so lose it, but let her lose her life for Jesus' sake so that she might find it.

O beloved, what will it profit you if you gain the whole world and forfeit your life? Or what shall you give in return for your life? For the Son of man is going to come with His angels in the glory of His Father, and then He will repay you according to what you have done.

Therefore, Father, cause her to continually consider Christ as more precious than life itself. For indeed He is! Remind her that unless she turns and becomes like a child, she will never enter the kingdom of heaven. Help her to constantly humble herself like a child, for such who do so are greatest in the kingdom of heaven. Amen (Matthew 16 & 18).

*All hell is vanquished when the believer bows his knee in importunate supplication. Beloved brethren, let us pray. We cannot all argue, but we can all pray; we cannot all be leaders, but we can all be pleaders; we cannot all be mighty in rhetoric, but we can all be prevalent in prayer. I would sooner see you eloquent with God than with men. Prayer links us with the Eternal, the Omnipotent, the Infinite, and hence it is our chief resort. . . . Be sure that you are with God, and then you may be sure that God is with you. ~Charles Spurgeon*

*Holy* Lord,

Compared to the rest of the world my wife is astonishingly rich. And only with difficulty will a rich person enter the kingdom of heaven. Therefore, if she will be saved, You must do what is impossible with man—give her a heart that cherishes You more than money, possessions, or comfort. Help her! For it is easier for a camel to go through the eye of a needle than for a rich person to enter Your kingdom. Praise be to Your name that with You all things are possible—that she and I can be saved!

Grant her the grace to leave houses or brothers or sisters or father or mother or children or lands, for the sake of Christ's name, so that she might receive a hundredfold and inherit eternal life. Amen (Matthew 19).

*S*oul-Satisfying God,

I desire true greatness for my lovely wife. May she seek to be a servant and slave, even as the Son of Man came not to be served but to serve, and to give His life as a ransom for many.

Please keep her loving You with all her heart and with all her soul and with all her mind. For that is the great and first commandment. And continue stirring her to love her neighbor as herself.

O Father, even as You grant her grace to adore You more, protect her from becoming a woman who preaches, but does not practice. May she never tie up heavy burdens, hard to bear, and lay them on people's shoulders, and then be unwilling to move them with her finger. Instead, enable her to humbly offer herself as their servant. Amen (Matthew 20 & 23).

*I have so much business I cannot get on
without spending three hours daily in prayer.* ~Martin Luther

ighteous Father,

There are so many pitfalls of hypocrisy that threaten to destroy my wonderful wife. You alone can guard her footsteps from straying from the narrow path. Let her never become one who does all her deeds to be seen by others, loving the place of honor at feasts and the admiration of churches and greetings in the marketplaces and being called wise by others.

O beloved, do not glory in your wisdom, for all you have is because of Jesus. For you have an instructor, the Christ. Whoever exalts herself will be humbled, and whoever humbles herself will be exalted.

Again, Father, may she never shut the kingdom of heaven in people's faces. Spare her from becoming a child of hell! Have mercy and save her from such woe (Matthew 23).

$\mathcal{O}$Thou who art beauty's fairest pleasure,

Protect my elegant wife. She dwells in a deceitful world; guard her mind. Keep her safe from blind guides and blind fools. Save her from following those who tithe generously and have neglected the weightier matters of the law: justice and mercy and faithfulness. May she not neglect these things, lest she be like the blind guides who strain out a gnat and swallow a camel!

Shield her also from the snare of merely external righteousness, like those who clean the outside of the cup and plate, but inside they are full of greed and self-indulgence. Please make her clean inside, that her outside also may be clean. Again, preserve her from becoming like a whitewashed tomb, which outwardly appears beautiful, but within is full of dead people's bones and all uncleanness. Woe to her if You do not rescue her from being one who outwardly appears righteous to others, but within is full of hypocrisy and lawlessness (Matthew 23).

*Prayer is designed by God to display his fullness and our need. Prayer glorifies God because it puts us in the position of the thirsty and God in the position of the all-supplying fountain.* ~John Piper

$\mathcal{M}$ighty Ruler,

Please, because of Christ, hear my prayer, and see that no one leads my precious wife astray. For many will come in Jesus' name, saying, "I am the Christ," and they will lead many astray. And when she hears of wars and rumors of wars, see that she is not alarmed.

O beloved, do not be surprised or afraid when kingdoms deliver us up to tribulation and put us to death. For the Son has warned us that we will be hated by all nations for His name's sake.

O Father, when many then fall away and betray one another and hate one another, let her not be one of them! Protect her from the many false prophets that will arise and lead many astray. And when lawlessness increases, do not let her love grow cold. But help her to endure to the end and be saved, and proclaim the gospel of the kingdom throughout the whole world as a testimony to all nations. Amen (Matthew 24).

## *W*insome Lord,

May my joy-instilling wife be like one of the wise virgins, who took flasks of oil with their lamps. So that when the cry comes at midnight, "Here is the bridegroom! Come out to meet Him," she may be ready to rise and go with Him to the marriage feast. Please keep her from being like the foolish virgins who took no oil, and so came late to the marriage feast. And finding the door shut, they were not allowed to enter.

O beloved, watch therefore, for you know neither the day nor the hour.

Again, Father, make her like the servants who doubled that with which their master had entrusted them before he went on a long journey. May she deal wisely with what You have given her, so that when You return You will say, "Well done, good and faithful servant. You have been faithful over a little; I will set you over much. Enter into the joy of your master." Keep her from being like the worthless, wicked, slothful servant who was cast into the outer darkness where there will be weeping and gnashing of teeth. Please preserve her by grace and wisdom.

Come quickly, Bridegroom and Master! Amen (Matthew 25).

*You cannot simply manipulate God by the power of being confident in what you ask. There are moral guidelines. This is what Jesus is saying with the condition, "If . . . my words abide in you, ask whatever you wish, and it will be done for you" (John 15:7). The words of Jesus shape the attitude and content of our prayers.* ~John Piper

*O*Lover of the sheep,

Only You can keep my wife for Jesus Christ when He comes in His glory and sits on His glorious throne. So I ask that You would preserve her as one of Your sheep, to whom the Son of Man will say on that day, "Come, you who are blessed by my Father, inherit the kingdom prepared for you from the foundation of the world."

May she be a woman who feeds the hungry, gives drink to the thirsty, welcomes the stranger, clothes the naked, and visits the sick and imprisoned.

O beloved, truly, I say to you, as you do it to one of the least of these, you do it to Christ.

Father, it is my fervent desire that she be such a righteous woman so that she might enter into eternal life. Thank You for the promise that, as she strives to enter by the narrow gate, Christ is with her always, to the end of the age.

Our great Saviour and King, we long for Your return. Amen (Matthew 25 & 28).

$\mathcal{L}$ord and Husband,

When my beloved wife strays from Your love, however wicked her waywardness proves to be, please draw her back! Even when she forgets You, allure her, and bring her into the wilderness, and speak tenderly to her. Make the Valley of Trouble a door of hope for her. May she answer You as in the days of her youth, as at the time when she came out of the land of bondage. And let her call You "My Husband." Make her lie down in safety and remind her that You have betrothed her to Yourself forever.

O beloved, forsake not your Husband! For He has betrothed you to Himself in righteousness and in justice, in steadfast love and in mercy. He has betrothed you to Himself in faithfulness. And you have known Him!

Father, be pleased to guard her from abandoning faithfulness, steadfast love, and the knowledge of You. Save her from being destroyed for lack of knowledge, from forsaking You to cherish whoredom, wine, and new wine, which take away the understanding. Preserve us both, for a people without understanding shall come to ruin (Hosea 2 & 4).

*Praying is the same to the new creature as crying is to the natural. The child is not learned by art or example to cry, but instructed by nature; it comes into the world crying. Praying is not a lesson got by forms and rules of art, but flowing from principles of new life itself.*
~William Gurnall

*R*edeeming Lover,

I thank You that, even when my wife played the whore and did not know You, and even as she stumbled in her guilt, You knew her, and her way was not hidden from You. Graciously You tore her that You might heal her; You struck her down, and You bound her wounds. Then You revived her and raised her up, that she might live before You. Praise be to You, LORD God! For You made her acknowledge her guilt and seek Your face. You caused her to turn to Yourself and to seek You earnestly in her distress.

O beloved, let us know; let us press on to know the LORD; His going out is sure as the dawn; He will come to us as the showers, as the spring rains that water the earth.

And now LORD God, let her not resemble Ephraim and Judah, whose love was like the morning cloud, like the dew that goes early away. Increase within her steadfast love for Your name. For You desire steadfast love and not sacrifice, the knowledge of God rather than burnt offerings. Prevent her from defiling herself with other lovers. And continue to restore her. Amen (Hosea 5, 6, 7).

*M*ost Holy Judge,

My precious wife is not immune to the subtle deceitfulness of sin. Therefore please protect her; increase her wisdom. Let her not be like a dove, silly and without sense. Woe to her if she strays from You! Only destruction will she find if You do not keep her.

May she never cry falsely, "My God, I—Your daughter—know You," when she has transgressed Your covenant and rebelled against Your law. Restrain her from making idols with her silver and gold. And forbid that she ever become incapable of innocence.

O beloved, cling to your righteous Husband! Fear the LORD and turn away from evil, lest you find yourself to be an useless vessel, and begin to regard His laws as a strange thing.

Father, may she not forget her Maker! Let her not grow to love a prostitute's wages. May she consecrate herself always to You and not to anything shameful, lest she become detestable like the thing she loves. Preserve her glory and righteousness, and do not give her a miscarrying womb and dry breasts. Accept her because she listens to You, and make her bear much fruit in Your house. Show Your love to her, that her children may see many days (Hosea 7, 8, 9).

*Cold prayers always freeze before they reach heaven.*
~Thomas Brooks

*M*erciful Leader of wayward children,

Thank You for growing my wife into a luxuriant vine that yields its fruit. You have dealt bountifully in giving her to me. But as her fruit increases, may she not use it to improve her pursuit of self or foreign altars. Guard her heart from becoming false, saying, "I have no king, for I do not fear the LORD." Such is the danger if You do not keep her. Unless You continue with her she will utter mere words; with empty oaths she will make covenants. Let her not be put to shame!

O beloved, He has kindly spared your fair neck. Do not make Him put you to the yoke to plow and harrow for yourself. Instead, sow for yourself righteousness; reap steadfast love.

LORD God, break up her fallow ground and let her seek You, that You may come and rain righteousness upon her.

Have mercy on us, for we have together plowed iniquity; we have reaped injustice; we have eaten the fruit of lies. We have trusted in our own way; do not destroy us! Because of our great evil we appeal to the righteousness of Christ, for apart from Him we should be dashed in pieces and utterly cut off.

O great Son of David, we praise Your Name and bow with trembling, thankful hearts. Hasten Your glorious return! Amen (Hosea 10).

*M*ost High Father,

Thank You that, when my exquisite wife was a child, You loved her, and out of Egypt You called Your daughter. Thank You for persisting, even when the more she was called, the more she went away and kept sacrificing to the gods of this world and burning offerings to self. Even so it was You who taught her to walk; You took her up by her arms, and now she knows that You healed her. Let her rejoice and sing for joy. For You led her with cords of kindness, with the bands of love, and You became to her as one who eases the yoke on her jaws, and You bent down to her and fed her.

O beloved, take care, and keep your soul diligently, lest you forget the things that your eyes have seen, and lest they depart from your heart all the days of your life.

Sovereign LORD, when her heart is bent on turning away from You, may Your compassion grow warm and tender. On account of Christ Jesus do not execute Your burning anger; for You are God and not a man, the Holy One in our midst, and because of Your great mercy do not come in wrath.

If she strays, roar like a lion, so that when You roar she shall come trembling; she shall return trembling like a bird from Egypt. Then may she walk with You and remain faithful to the Holy One (Hosea 11 & Deuteronomy 4).

*I had rather learn what some men really judge about their own justification from their prayers than their writings.* ~John Owen

$\mathcal{L}$ORD God of hosts,

May my breathtaking wife, by Your help, hold fast to love and justice, and wait continually for You. Keep her from incurring guilt and forsaking Christ. For if she does she shall be like the morning mist or like the dew that goes early away, like the chaff that swirls from the threshing floor or like smoke from a window. You are the LORD our God; we know no God but You, and besides You there is no savior. It was You who knew her in the wilderness, in the land of drought. But now, when she is filled, and her heart is lifted up, let her not forget You.

Even when she turns away from her Helper, because of Christ, do not destroy her. I thank You for His sacrifice on her behalf, so that You will not devour her and rip her open in Your wrath.

O beloved, bless the Name of Jesus, for He has ransomed you from the power of Sheol! He has redeemed you from Death. O Death, where are your plagues? O Sheol, where is your sting? The sting of death is sin, and the power of sin is the law. But thanks be to God, who gives us the victory through our Lord Jesus Christ.

LORD God, let not compassion be hidden from Your eyes toward her. May she flourish among her sisters, and may her fountain never dry up. Amen (Hosea 12, 13, I Corinthians 15).

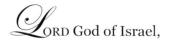ORD God of Israel,

Continue in faithful mercy toward my most treasured wife.
Turn Your anger from her and love her freely. Be like the dew to
her, causing her to blossom like the lily, and take root like the
trees of Lebanon. Then her shoots shall spread out; her beauty
shall be like the olive, and her fragrance like Lebanon. Let her
dwell beneath Your shadow; may she flourish like the grain and
blossom like the vine; make her fame be like the wine of Lebanon.

O beloved, what has our LORD God to do with idols? It is He
who answers and looks after you. He is like an evergreen cypress;
from Him comes your fruit.

Sovereign LORD, let her be wise and understand these things;
give her discernment to know them; for Your ways are right, and
the upright walk in them, but transgressors stumble in them
(Hosea 14).

*In God's commands to pray, we are compelled by the force of divine
authority to come and drink of the living water, to receive bread from
heaven, and to realize afresh moment by moment by moment that all
that we long for, and everything that is good, is found in one and only
one place: in God.* ~Bruce Ware

$\mathcal{L}$ORD of Zion,

Thank You that through Christ my lovely wife is washed; she is made clean; the evil of her deeds is removed from before Your eyes because He has borne her punishment. Assist her now to cease to do evil, learn to do good, seek justice, correct oppression, bring justice to the fatherless, plead the widow's cause.

Come now, beloved, let us reason together: though your sins were like scarlet, they are now white as snow; though they were red like crimson, they have now become like wool. Trust Christ for your righteousness! He is a great Saviour.

Come, LORD God, and lead her up to Your mountain, to the house of the God of Jacob, that You may teach her Your ways and that she may walk in Your paths. O LORD, let her walk in Your light.

Let her stop regarding man in whose nostrils is breath, for of what account is he? Instead, give her more regard for Christ, so that on the day of the LORD she will not need to hide in the dust from before Your terror, and from the splendor of Your majesty. Prepare us together for that day, when the haughty looks of man shall be brought low, and the lofty pride of men shall be humbled, and You alone will be exalted (Isaiah 1 & 2).

Eternal Source of all good,

Please continue to restrain the wicked inclinations that remain in my wife's heart. For if You do not, she will soon become haughty and walk with an outstretched neck, glancing wantonly with her eyes. Go on with Your work of making her holy, washing away the filth of Your daughter, and cleansing her bloodstains by a spirit of purging.

Thank You for loving her as a choice vineyard, and planting her with choice vines on a fertile hill. Now let her yield grapes, and not wild grapes.

O beloved, you are the LORD's pleasant planting. Therefore, do not feast with tambourine and flute and wine, and disregard the deeds of the LORD, or turn a blind eye to the work of His hands.

LORD of hosts, let her never be found lacking in the knowledge of You, so that she may not condemn herself to exile, hunger, and thirst. For before You man is humbled, and each one is brought low, and the eyes of the haughty are brought low. But You are exalted in justice, and You show Yourself holy in righteousness (Isaiah 3, 4, 5).

*I have been benefited by praying for others; for by making an errand to God for them I have gotten something for myself.* ~Samuel Rutherford

$\mathcal{L}$ORD of hosts,

Guard my tender wife from those who draw iniquity with cords of falsehood, who draw sin as with cart ropes. Protect her from those who call evil good and good evil, who put darkness for light and light for darkness, who put bitter for sweet and sweet for bitter! There are many who are wise in their own eyes, and shrewd in their own sight; let her not be found among them. Make her stand firm and humble in the midst of those who are heroes at drinking wine, who acquit the guilty for a bribe, and deprive the innocent of his right. For they have rejected Your law, and have despised the word of the Holy One of Israel. Therefore, their root will be as rottenness, and their blossom will go up like dust.

O beloved, sing with me the words of the seraphim. "Holy, holy, holy is the LORD of hosts; the whole earth is full of His glory!" Behold, through Christ your guilt is taken away, and your sin atoned for. Therefore, you can now rejoice when your eyes see the King, the LORD of hosts.

Help her to remain firm in faith, O LORD. For if she is not firm in faith, she will not be firm at all. And let her not fear what the world fears, nor be in dread. But You, O LORD of hosts—may she regard You as holy. May You be her fear, and may You be her dread. Amen (Isaiah 5, 6, 7, 8).

$\mathcal{O}$mniscient Father,

Thank You that my dearest wife who walked in darkness has seen a great light; she used to dwell in a land of deep darkness, but now on her light has shined. Please multiply her fruit; increase her joy; may she rejoice before You as with joy at the harvest, as those who are glad when they divide great spoil. For the yoke of her burden, and the staff for her shoulder, and the rod of her oppressor, You have broken as on the day of Midian. For to us a child was born, to her the Son was given; and the government is upon His shoulder, and His name is called Wonderful Counselor, Mighty God, Everlasting Father, Prince of Peace.

O beloved, let us adore our great Saviour! Of the increase of His government and of peace there will be no end. He has established it and upholds it with justice and with righteousness from this time forth and forevermore.

O LORD of hosts, thank You that Your zeal has accomplished salvation for her through Christ. Amen (Isaiah 9).

*In personal relationships, if we attempt to fake emotional intensity and put on an outward show of emotion that is not consistent with the feelings of our hearts, others involved will usually sense our hypocrisy at once and be put off by it. How much more is this true of God, who fully knows our hearts. Therefore, intensity and depth of emotional involvement in prayer should never be faked: we cannot fool God.*
~Wayne Grudem

$\mathscr{M}$ajestic One,

In this day let my beautiful wife lean on You, the Holy One of Israel, in truth. Please continue to change her into the likeness of the shoot that came forth from the stump of Jesse. May Your Spirit rest upon her, the Spirit of wisdom and understanding, the Spirit of counsel and might, the Spirit of knowledge and the fear of the LORD. And let her delight be always in the fear of You. Clothe her with righteousness as the belt of her waist, and faithfulness as the belt of her loins.

I will give thanks to You, O LORD, for though You were once angry with her, Your anger turned away because of Christ, that You might comfort her.

O beloved, God is your salvation; trust, and do not be afraid; for the LORD GOD is your strength and your song, and He has become your salvation!

Therefore, O God, cause her to draw water from the wells of salvation with joy. And may she give thanks to You, call upon Your name, make known Your deeds among the peoples, and proclaim that Your name is exalted. May she sing praises to You, for You have done gloriously; let her make this known in all the earth. Let us shout together and sing for joy, for great in our midst are You, O Holy One of Israel (Isaiah 10, 11, 12).

$\mathcal{S}$overeign, eternal, unchangeable LORD,

You are my God; I will exalt You; I will praise Your name, for You have done wonderful things, plans formed of old, faithful and sure. For You have made my elegant wife; she is the work of Your hands. Let her glorify You; let her fear You. May You be to her a stronghold; a stronghold when she is needy and in distress, her shelter from the storm and her shade from the heat.

May she hope and long for the day when You will make for all peoples a feast of rich food, a feast of well-aged wine, of rich food full of marrow, of aged wine well refined.

O beloved, on that day He will swallow up death forever; and the Lord GOD will wipe away tears from all faces, and the reproach of His people He will take away from all the earth, for the LORD has spoken.

You are our God; we have waited for You, that You might save us. You are the LORD; together we have waited for You; let us be glad and rejoice in Your salvation. Keep her in perfect peace because her mind is stayed on You, because she trusts in You. Help her to trust in You forever, for You are an everlasting rock (Isaiah 25 & 26).

*You should, in Tertullian's phrase, with a holy conspiracy, besiege heaven.* ~Thomas Manton

 LORD my God,

Please make level the path of my glorious wife; for You make
the way of the righteous level. In the path of Your judgments, O
LORD, let her wait for You; may Your name and remembrance be
the desire of her soul. Make her soul yearn for You in the night;
cause her spirit within her to earnestly seek You. For when Your
judgments are in the earth, the inhabitants of the world learn
righteousness.

O LORD, ordain peace for her; do for her all her works. Even
though other lords besides You may rule over her, let her bring
Your name alone to remembrance.

You have made her a pleasant vineyard, a vineyard of wine; I
will sing of her! Let her trust You, for You, the LORD, are her
keeper; every moment You water her. You keep her night and day;
may she lay hold of Your protection. In the days to come let her
blossom and put forth shoots and fill the whole world with fruit.
Amen (Isaiah 26 & 27).

$\mathcal{L}$ORD of power,

Please be to my sweet wife a crown of glory and a diadem of beauty. For You are the LORD of hosts, wonderful in counsel and excellent in wisdom.

Protect her from hypocrisy. May it never be that she draw near with her mouth and honor You with her lips, while her heart is far from You. Let her fear of You be genuine, and not a commandment taught by men.

O beloved, guard your heart, lest you turn things upside down and regard the Potter as the clay.

O LORD, keep her from saying of her Maker, "He did not make me"; or of You who formed her, "He has no understanding." Instead, let her be turned into a fruitful field. Out of her gloom and darkness cause her to see and obtain fresh joy in You. May she exult in You, the Holy One of Israel, and no more be ashamed. Let her see the work of Your hands and sanctify Your name; let her sanctify the Holy One of Jacob and stand in awe of the God of Israel (Isaiah 28 & 29).

*Just as God's Word must reform our theology, our ethics, and our practices, so also must it reform our praying.* ~D.A. Carson

$\mathcal{E}$xalted Fountain of Grace,

May my delicate wife find her strength in quietness and in trust, for You wait to be gracious to her. Therefore, exalt Yourself to show mercy to her. For You are a God of justice; blessed are all those who wait for You. Gather her into Your arms so that she will weep no more.

O beloved, He will surely be gracious to you at the sound of your cry. As soon as He hears it, He answers you.

Let her trust Your promise, O LORD, that though You give her the bread of adversity and the water of affliction, yet You will not hide Yourself forever, but her eyes shall see her Teacher. And may her ears hear a word behind her, saying, "This is the way, walk in it," when she turns to the right or when she turns to the left. Let her also defile her idols of the flesh, and scatter them as unclean things, saying to them, "Be gone!"

Cause her hope to remain rooted and steadfast in You when calamity overtakes her. For soon the light of the moon will be as the light of the sun, and the light of the sun will be sevenfold, as the light of seven days, in the day when You bind up the brokenness of Your people, and heal the wounds inflicted by Your blow. With Your burning anger devour her enemies, and give her a song as in the night when a holy feast is kept, and gladness of heart, as when one sets out to the sound of the flute to go to the mountain of the LORD, to the Rock of Israel. Cause Your majestic voice to be heard by her. Amen (Isaiah 30).

*W*orker of wonders,

Continue to make my wife righteous, so that she may have peace, quietness, and security forever. O LORD, be gracious to her; I wait for You. Be her arm every morning, her salvation in the time of trouble. For You are exalted, for You dwell on high; fill her with justice and righteousness, and be the stability of her days, abundance of salvation, wisdom, and knowledge; let the fear of You be her treasure. Arise, O LORD, lift Yourself up; be exalted in her.

Help her to become a woman who walks righteously and speaks uprightly, who despises the gain of oppressions, who shakes her hands, lest they hold a bribe, who stops her ears from hearing of bloodshed and shuts her eyes from looking on evil. Then she will dwell on the heights; her place of defense will be the fortress of rocks; her bread will be given her; her water will be sure.

Let her eyes behold You in Your beauty. Be with her in majesty, for You are her judge; You are her lawgiver; You are her king; You will save her (Isaiah 32 & 33).

*One cannot begin to face the real difficulties of the life of prayer and meditation unless one is first perfectly content to be a beginner and really experience himself as one who knows little or nothing and has a desperate need to learn the bare rudiments. Those who think they "know" from the beginning will never, in fact, come to know anything.*
~Thomas Merton

eautiful LORD,

Let my precious wife be glad as she looks to the day of the Son's return. May she rejoice and blossom like the crocus; let her blossom abundantly and rejoice with joy and singing. And may she long to see Your glory, the majesty of her God. Strengthen her weak hands, and make firm her feeble knees.

O beloved, be not anxious of heart. Be strong; fear not! Behold, your God will come with vengeance, with the recompense of God. He will come and save you. Then the eyes of the blind shall be opened, and the ears of the deaf unstopped; then shall the lame man leap like a deer, and the tongue of the mute sing for joy.

Prepare her, O LORD, to set foot on the great highway, which shall be called the Way of Holiness; for the unclean shall not pass over it. It shall belong to those who walk on the way; let her not go astray. Let her yearn for that day when the redeemed shall walk there, when the ransomed of the LORD shall return and come to Zion with singing. Everlasting joy shall be upon their heads; they shall obtain gladness and joy, and sorrow and sighing shall flee away (Isaiah 35).

*God can pick sense out of a confused prayer.* ~Richard Sibbes

$\mathcal{O}$LORD of hosts, God of Israel,

enthroned above the cherubim, You are the God, You alone, of all the kingdoms of the earth; You have made heaven and earth; You have made my exquisite wife. Incline Your ear, O LORD, and hear; open Your eyes, O LORD, and see; and hear all the words of those who mock You, the living God. Truly, O LORD, there are many who desire to lay waste all the fruit of my wife's hands. In their wickedness they have destroyed others and cast their gods into the fire—the work of men's hands, wood and stone. So now, O LORD my God, save her from their hands, that all the kingdoms of the earth may know that You alone are the LORD. Please defend her to save her, for Your own sake.

Please, O LORD, remember her and cause her to walk before You in faithfulness and with a whole heart, and to do what is good in Your sight. May she trust that it is for her welfare when she has great bitterness; let her praise You and hope for Your faithfulness.

O beloved, in love He has delivered your life from the pit of destruction, for He has cast all your sins behind His back.

Let her thank You, O LORD, as I do this day; let her make known to her children Your faithfulness. For it is You who will save us, and we will play music on stringed instruments all the days of our lives, at the house of the LORD (Isaiah 37 & 38).

$\mathcal{W}$onderful God,

Comfort, comfort my dear wife. Speak tenderly to her and cry to her that her iniquity is pardoned, that because of Christ she has not received from Your hand double for all her sins. May she wait patiently for the day when Your glory shall be revealed, and all flesh shall see it together, for You have spoken.

O beloved, all flesh is grass, and all its beauty is like the flower of the field. The grass withers, the flower fades when the breath of the LORD blows on it; surely the people are grass. The grass withers, the flower fades, but the word of our God will stand forever.

Lord GOD, let her behold You coming with might; with Your arm ruling for You. Please tend her like a shepherd; gather her into Your arms; carry her in Your bosom, and gently lead her.

May she worship You as the only one who has measured the waters in the hollow of his hand and marked off the heavens with a span, enclosed the dust of the earth in a measure and weighed the mountains in scales and the hills in a balance. We praise You, for no man has directed Your Spirit or shown You his counsel. Amen (Isaiah 40).

*As highly as Paul values marital obligations, he can envisage a couple self-consciously choosing not to have sex together for a while, so that the time they would have spent pleasing each other sexually will be devoted to prayer. That says something about Paul's valuation of prayer. ~D. A. Carson*

Creator of the ends of the earth,

Be exalted in Your wisdom and fullness, for You have never needed anyone. Whom did You consult, and who made You understand? Who taught You the path of justice, and taught You knowledge, and showed You the way of understanding? Behold, the nations are like a drop from a bucket, and are accounted as the dust on the scales; behold, You take up the coastlands like fine dust. Lebanon would not suffice for fuel, nor are its beasts enough for a burnt offering. All the nations are as nothing before You, they are accounted by You as less than nothing and emptiness.

Therefore, let my treasured wife worship and adore Your greatness, taking comfort that You are powerful and lack nothing.

O beloved, to whom then will you liken God, or what likeness compare with Him? You have known and heard, and it has been told you from the beginning, that it is He who sits above the circle of the earth, and its inhabitants are like grasshoppers; who stretches out the heavens like a curtain, and spreads them like a tent to dwell in; who brings princes to nothing, and makes the rulers of the earth as emptiness.

O Holy One, to whom then will we compare You, that You should be like him? Lift up our eyes on high to see: You created the stars—You who bring out their host by number, calling them all by name, by the greatness of Your might, and because You are strong in power not one is missing (Isaiah 40).

$\mathcal{Y}$ou who alone are the true God,

May my graceful wife never complain that her way is hidden from You, or that her right is disregarded by her God. Instead, assure her that You are the everlasting God, the Creator of the ends of the earth. Instill within her a steadfast confidence in You, for You do not faint or grow weary; Your understanding is unsearchable. Give power to her when she is faint, and when she has no might increase her strength. Even when she faints and becomes weary, when she falls exhausted, let her wait on You. For they who wait for You shall renew their strength; they shall mount up with wings like eagles; they shall run and not be weary; they shall walk and not faint.

Thank You for choosing her, for taking her from the pit, for calling her out of bondage, saying to her, "You are my servant, I have chosen you and not cast you off."

O beloved, fear not, for He is with you; be not dismayed, for He is your God; He will strengthen, He will help you, He will uphold you with His righteous right hand.

O LORD my God, hold her right hand, and say to her, "Fear not, I am the one who helps you" (Isaiah 40 & 41).

*Intercession is more than specific: it is pondered: it requires us to bear on our heart the burden of those for whom we pray.*
~George A. Buttrick

*K*ing of Jacob,

Defend my priceless wife from all who are incensed against her; let them be put to shame and confounded; may those who strive against her be as nothing and perish. Let the evil ones who war against her be as nothing at all.

Fear not, beloved, you glorious gift of God! He is the one who helps you; your Redeemer is the Holy One of Israel.

O LORD, let her rejoice in You; in the Holy One of Israel let her glory. When she is poor and needy and seeks for water, and there is none, and her tongue is parched with thirst, please answer her; O God of Israel, do not forsake her. Open rivers on the bare heights, and fountains in the midst of the valleys. Make the wilderness a pool of water, and the dry land springs of water for her. Put in her wilderness the cedar, the acacia, the myrtle, and the olive. Set in her desert the cypress, the plane and the pine together, that she may see and know, may consider and understand, that Your hand has done it, the Holy One of Israel has created it.

Increase her soul's delight in Your Servant, whom You uphold, Your chosen, just as Your soul delights in Him. May she hope in Him, for a bruised reed He will not break, and a faintly burning wick He will not quench; He will faithfully bring forth justice. Hasten the day of His return! Amen (Isaiah 41 & 42).

$\mathcal{O}$God, the LORD,

who created the heavens and stretched them out, who spread out the earth and what comes from it, who gives breath to the people on it and spirit to those who walk in it, reassure my adorable wife that You are the LORD, and have called her in righteousness. Take her by the hand and keep her. Conform her into the image of Him who is given as a covenant for the people, a light for the nations, to open the eyes that are blind, to bring out the prisoners from the dungeon, from the prison those who sit in darkness.

O beloved, pursue Christ! Esteem Christ! Honor His Father, for He is the LORD; that is His name; His glory He gives to no other, nor His praise to carved idols.

Let her sing to You a new song, O LORD, Your praise from the end of the earth. Let her lift up her voice along with the sea, and all that fills it, the coastlands and their inhabitants, the desert and its cities. May she sing for joy, and shout from the top of the mountains. Let her give glory to You, and declare Your praise in the coastlands. For You go out like a mighty man, like a man of war You stir up Your zeal; You cry out, You shout aloud, You show Yourself mighty against Your foes.

Lead her in a way that she does not know, in paths that she has not known please guide her. Turn the darkness before her into light, the rough places into level ground. For these are the things that You do, and You will not forsake her (Isaiah 42).

$\mathcal{H}$oly LORD,

Be pleased, for Your righteousness' sake, to magnify Your law and make it glorious through my wife. Be exalted, for You created her, You formed her. May she fear not, for You have redeemed her; You have called her by name, she is Yours. When she passes through the waters, please be with her; and through the rivers, let them not overwhelm her; when she walks through fire let her not be burned, and may the flame not consume her. For You are the LORD her God, the Holy One of Israel, her Savior.

O beloved, because you are precious in His eyes, and honored, and He loves you, He gives men in return for you, peoples in exchange for your life. Fear not, for He is with you. He is the LORD, and besides Him there is no savior.

Let her adore You as the LORD, her Redeemer, her Holy One, the Creator of Israel, her King. Give water to her in the wilderness, rivers when she is in the desert, to give drink to Your chosen daughter, the woman whom You formed for Yourself that she might declare Your praise. Thank You that You are He who blots out her transgressions for Your own sake, and You will not remember her sins. For she is Your servant whom You have chosen; You made her and formed her from the womb. Help her, and let her not fear. Pour Your Spirit upon her offspring, and Your blessing on her descendants. Let them spring up among the grass like willows by flowing streams. May one say, "I am the LORD's,' and another write on his hand, "The LORD's," and name himself by the name of Israel (Isaiah 42, 43, 44).

$\mathcal{K}$ing and Redeemer of Israel,

Glory be to Your name, for You are the first and You are the last; besides You there is no god. Who is like You? Therefore, let my wife not fear, nor be afraid; for You declare what is to come, and what will happen. May she trust in You, for there is no god besides You, there is no Rock; I know not any.

Let her remember that all who fashion idols are nothing, and the things they delight in do not profit, for she is Your servant; You formed her; she is Your servant; let her not be forgotten by You.

O beloved, He has blotted out your transgressions like a cloud and your sins like mist; cling to Him, for He has redeemed you!

Sing, O heavens, for the LORD has done it; shout, O depths of the earth; break forth into singing, O mountains, O forest, and every tree in it! For You, LORD, have redeemed my wife, and will be glorified in her. Through her be pleased to display Your beauty.

May she take comfort and rejoice in the knowledge that You formed her in the womb, that You are the LORD, who made all things, who alone stretched out the heavens, who spread out the earth by Yourself, who frustrates the signs of liars and makes fools of diviners, who turns wise men back and makes their knowledge foolish, who says to the deep, "Be dry; I will dry up your rivers." Let her love and fear You. Amen (Isaiah 44).

*All progress in prayer is an answer to prayer—our own or another's. And all true prayer promotes its own progress and increases our power to pray. ~P. T. Forsyth*

$\mathcal{L}$ORD God of Israel, who calls His people by name,

I come before You on behalf of my dearest wife because You are the LORD, and there is no other, besides You there is no God. Please equip her to make known Your might, that people may know, from the rising of the sun and from the west, that there is none besides You; You are the LORD, and there is no other. May she tremble and rejoice at the truth that You form light and create darkness. Let her worship and bow down before You as the one who makes well-being and creates calamity. May she exalt You as the LORD who does all these things.

O beloved, praise and adore Him with me! For He made the earth and created man on it; it was His hands that stretched out the heavens, and He commanded all their host.

Stir her up, O LORD, in righteousness, and make all her ways level. May the wealthy and men of stature come to her, saying, "Surely God is in you, and there is no other, no god besides Him."

Many women make idols and go in confusion together. But I thank You that my wife is saved by You with everlasting salvation; she shall not be put to shame or confounded to all eternity. For You are the LORD and there is no other. You did not say to her, "Seek me in vain." You speak truth; You declare what is right (Isaiah 45).

*O* God who hears prayer,

Let my wife turn continually to You for her salvation. For You are God, and there is no other. Therefore let her say of You, "Only in the LORD are righteousness and strength." Thank You that in You she is justified and glories. Praise be to Your name, for she has been borne by You from before her birth, carried from the womb; even to her old age You are He, and to gray hairs You will carry her. You have made, and You will bear; You will carry and will save.

O beloved, remember with me that He is God, and there is no other; He is God, and there is none like Him, declaring the end from the beginning and from ancient times things not yet done, saying, "My counsel shall stand, and I will accomplish all my purpose."

Therefore, great LORD, may she trust the word that goes out from Your mouth in righteousness. Let her hope in You as the God who brings to pass what He speaks; who does what He has purposed. For Your name's sake be gracious to her, for the sake of Your praise make her walk in holiness, and do not cut her off. Refine her, and give her strength as You try her in the furnace of affliction. For Your own sake, for Your own sake, do this, for how should Your name be profaned? Your glory You will not give to another. Therefore magnify Yourself in her! Glorify Yourself through her! Use her to exalt the greatness of Your name. Amen (Isaiah 45, 46, 48).

*My* Redeemer,

Teach my beautiful wife to profit from uprightness, and lead her in the way she should go. Make her pay attention to Your commandments so that her peace will be like a river, and her righteousness like the waves of the sea; then let her offspring be like the sand, and her descendents like its grains; may their name never be cut off or destroyed from before You.

Now, even now I shout for joy, for You have redeemed her! Therefore do not let her thirst when You lead her through deserts; make water flow for her even from the rocks, so that her soul is satisfied.

Make her mouth like a sharp sword; in the shadow of Your hand please hide her; make her a polished arrow; in Your quiver hide her away.

O beloved, you are the LORD's servant, in whom He will be glorified and display His beauty. You have not labored in vain; you have not spent your strength for nothing. For surely your recompense is with your God.

I will praise You, O LORD, for You called her from the womb, from the body of her mother You named her name. You formed her from the womb to be Your servant, therefore may she be honored in Your eyes, and may You continually be her strength. Make her as a light for the nations, that Your salvation may reach to the ends of the earth. Let kings see and arise; may princes prostrate themselves; because of You, who are faithful, the Holy One of Israel, who has chosen her (Isaiah 48 & 49).

$\mathcal{R}$uler of heaven and earth,

Please keep my precious wife. Answer her and help her; let her not hunger or thirst, and may neither scorching wind nor sun strike her. Have pity on her and lead her, and by springs of water guide her.

Sing for joy, O heavens, and exult, O earth; break forth, O mountains, into singing! for the LORD has comforted my beloved and will have compassion on her affliction.

I praise You that You have not forsaken her; You have not forgotten her. Even a woman may forget her nursing child, yet You will not forget my wife. Assure her of this, and let her know that You are the LORD; those who wait for You shall not be put to shame. Fight for her; contend with those who contend with her. Then all flesh shall know that You are the LORD her Savior, and her Redeemer, the Mighty One of Jacob (Isaiah 49).

*The artless child is still the divine model for all of us. Prayer will increase in power and reality as we repudiate all pretense and learn to be utterly honest before God as well as before men.* ~A. W. Tozer

orgiving God,

Thank You that Your hand is not shortened, that it can redeem my dear wife. For by Your power and rebuke You dry up the sea, and make the rivers a desert.

Please give her the tongue of those who are taught, that she may know how to sustain with a word those who are weary. Morning by morning awaken her; awaken her ear to hear as those who are taught.

When she is struck and spit upon for Your namesake fill her with hope in You, the Lord GOD. For You will help her; therefore she will not be disgraced. Remind her that she will not be put to shame, for You who vindicate her are near.

Let her fear You and obey the voice of Your servant, Christ. And when she walks in darkness and has no light let her trust in Your name and rely on her God. Cause her to pursue righteousness and seek You. Make her wilderness like Eden, her desert like the garden of the LORD; may joy and gladness be found in her, thanksgiving and the voice of song (Isaiah 50 & 51).

*Prayer is often represented as the great means of the Christian life. But it is no mere means, it is the great end of that life. It is, of course, not untrue to call it a means. It is so, especially at first. But at last it is truer to say that we live the Christian life in order to pray than that we pray in order to live the Christian life.* ~P. T. Forsyth

$\mathcal{L}$ovely God,

Turn the attention of my sweet wife to Yourself. Let her give ear to the law that has gone out from You, to the justice that You have set for a light to the peoples. May Your righteousness draw near to her, let Your salvation go out to her; make her hope for You, and for Your arm let her wait.

Lift up her eyes to the heavens, and cause her to look at the earth beneath and see that the heavens vanish like smoke, the earth will wear out like a garment, and they who dwell in it will die in like manner. But remind her that Your salvation will be forever, and Your righteousness will never be dismayed.

Listen to Him, O beloved, you who know righteousness; for He says, "Fear not the reproach of man, nor be dismayed at their revilings. For the moth will eat them up like a garment, and the worm will eat them like wool; but my righteousness will be forever, and my salvation to all generations."

Awake, awake, put on strength, O arm of the LORD; awake, as in days of old, the generations of long ago, and defend my wife. You have ransomed her, therefore let her come into Your presence with singing; crown her head with everlasting joy; grant her gladness and joy, so that sorrow and sighing shall flee away.

Teach her to not be afraid of man who dies, of the son of man who is made like grass, for You, You are He who comforts her. Let her take confidence in You, her Maker, who stretched out the heavens and laid the foundations of the earth, and may she fear not the oppressors who set themselves up to destroy (Isaiah 51).

$\mathcal{L}$ord of the oceans,

who stirs up the sea so that its waves roar, please put Your words in my wife's mouth and cover her in the shadow of Your hand. For You are the LORD of hosts, who established the heavens and laid the foundations of the earth, and say to her, "You are my daughter."

Thank You for awakening her from the slumber of death, for clothing her with strength and beautiful garments. For she was sold for nothing, and You have redeemed her without money. Therefore make her feet beautiful upon the mountains, as one who brings good news, who publishes peace, who brings good news of happiness, who publishes salvation, who says, "My God reigns." Let her lift up her voice with me, so that together we may sing for joy, and eye to eye await the return of Your Son.

O beloved, let us break forth together into singing, for the LORD has comforted His people; He has redeemed even us! The LORD has bared His holy arm before the eyes of all the nations, and all the ends of the earth shall see the salvation of our God.

LORD, please go always before her; O God of Israel, be her rear guard. Amen (Isaiah 51 & 52).

*When our awareness of the greatness of God and the gospel is dim, our prayer lives will be small. The less we think of the nature and character of God, and the less we are reminded of what Jesus did for us on the Cross, the less we want to pray.* ~Donald S. Whitney

$\mathcal{My}$ Father and my God,

Grow within the heart of my wonderful wife a deep esteem for Him who has borne her griefs and carried her sorrows, who was wounded for her transgressions and crushed for her iniquities. May she treasure Him increasingly, desire Him more fervently, for upon Him was the chastisement that brought her peace, and with His stripes she is healed.

Let her love and cherish Him as the One stricken for her transgression. May she praise You with trembling for crushing Him so that she could be accounted righteous. Stir up gratitude within her for His sacrifice, for bearing her iniquities, pouring out His soul to death, and for making intercession for her.

Sing, O beloved! Break forth into singing and cry aloud! For you have been reconciled to your Maker and Husband, to the LORD of hosts; the Holy of One of Israel is your Redeemer!

O LORD, thank You for calling her when she was like a wife deserted and grieved in spirit. And now be exalted for Your great compassion toward her! Keep her in Your sovereign arms. Amen (Isaiah 53 & 54).

*G*od of the whole earth,

Do not hide Your beautiful face from my wife or be angry with her, but with everlasting love have compassion on her. Even though the mountains may depart and the hills be removed, let not Your steadfast love depart from her, and do not remove Your covenant of peace, but continue to have compassion on her.

O beloved, although you may be afflicted and storm-tossed, take comfort in His word! For behold, He will set your stones in antimony, and lay your foundations with sapphires. He will wall you in with precious stones.

LORD, bless her, and may all her children be taught by You, and let the peace of her children be great. Establish her in righteousness; keep her far from oppression and fear. Protect her from terror; may it not come near her. I commit her to Your hand, for You guard her so that no weapon that is fashioned against her shall succeed (Isaiah 54).

*Meditation is a middle sort of duty between the word and prayer, and hath respect to both. The word feedeth meditation, and meditation feedeth prayer. These duties must always go hand in hand; meditation must follow hearing and precede prayer. To hear and not to meditate is unfruitful. We may hear and hear, but it is like putting a thing into a bag with holes.... It is rashness to pray and not to meditate. What we take in by the word we digest by meditation and let out by prayer. These three duties must be ordered that one may not jostle out the other. Men are barren, dry, and sapless in their prayers for want of exercising themselves in holy thoughts.* ~ Thomas Manton

$\mathcal{C}$ompassionate LORD,

When my tender wife thirsts, draw her to the waters, draw her to Yourself. Keep her from spending her money for that which is not bread, and her labor for that which does not satisfy. Instead, make her listen diligently to You, and eat what is good, and delight herself in rich food—wine and milk without price. Incline her ear, and let her come to You; may she hear, that her soul may live, because of Your everlasting covenant of steadfast, sure love.

O beloved, seek the LORD while He may be found; call upon Him while He is near! Let us forsake our wicked ways and our unrighteous thoughts; and let us turn to the LORD, that He may have compassion on us, and to our God, for He will abundantly pardon.

Holy One of Israel, we bow together before You, for Your thoughts are not our thoughts, neither are Your ways our ways. We worship and exalt You, for as the heavens are higher than the earth, so are Your ways higher than our ways and Your thoughts than our thoughts. Amen (Isaiah 55).

*Y*ou who are high and lifted up,

Be pleased to fill my treasured wife with joy and lead her forth in peace. May she keep justice, and do righteousness, for Your salvation has come, and Your deliverance is revealed. Keep her hand from doing any evil, and make her hold on to righteousness.

Thank You for saving her; for giving her an everlasting name that shall not be cut off. Let the mountains and the hills break forth into singing, and all the trees of the field clap their hands! For You have made a name for Yourself; You have redeemed her! Make her joyful in Your house of prayer.

Please protect her from blind watchmen without knowledge, from shepherds who have no understanding. Revive her spirit when she is lowly, and revive her heart when she is contrite. May she seek You daily and delight to know Your ways; let her delight to draw near to You. And when she fasts, may it not be merely to quarrel and pursue her own business. But cause her to fast as You choose: to loose the bonds of wickedness, to undo the straps of the yoke, to let the oppressed go free, to share her bread with the hungry, to bring the homeless poor into her house, and to clothe the naked. Then may her light break forth like the dawn, and make righteousness go before her, with Your glory as her rear guard (Isaiah 55, 56, 58).

*A chief object of all prayer is to bring us to God....*
*The chief failure of prayer is its cessation.* ~P. T. Forsyth

*Y*ou who inhabit eternity,

When I call to You, please answer. I cry out to You on behalf of my dearest wife. Keep her from speaking wickedness. But rather, may she pour herself out for the hungry and satisfy the desire of the afflicted, for then shall her light rise in the darkness and her gloom be as the noonday. Guide her continually and satisfy her desire in scorched places and make her bones strong; may she be like a watered garden, like a spring of water, whose waters do not fail. Let her take delight in You; feed her with the heritage of Jacob.

O beloved, arise, shine, for your light has come, and the glory of the LORD has risen upon you. Although darkness once covered you, now the LORD has risen upon you, and His glory is seen upon you. And nations shall come to your light, and kings to the brightness of Christ in you!

LORD God, may peoples see her and be radiant; let their hearts thrill and exult because of the abundance of her joy in Christ. Make her declare the good news—the praises of Christ. Beautify your beautiful servant so that the coastlands will hope for You, for the name of the LORD her God, and for the Holy One of Israel, because You have made her beautiful (Isaiah 58 & 60).

$\mathcal{O}$God whose name is Holy,

In Your favor be pleased to have mercy on my beautiful wife. Make her majestic forever, and a joy to every age, so that all may know that You, the LORD, are her Savior and her Redeemer, the Mighty One of Jacob. Make her overseers peace and her taskmasters righteousness. May her clothing be called Salvation, and the gates to her house Praise.

O beloved, trust in the LORD, and He will be your everlasting light, and your God will be your glory! Seek His face, and He will be your beauty.

LORD, let her hope in You as her everlasting light. Clothe her with righteousness that You may be glorified. Use her to display Your beauty.

Please comfort her when she mourns; give her the oil of gladness instead of mourning, the garment of praise instead of a faint spirit; that she may be called an oak of righteousness, the planting of the LORD, that You may be glorified. Let her greatly rejoice in You; let her soul exult in her God, for You have clothed her with the garments of salvation; You have covered her with the robe of righteousness, as a bride adorns herself with her jewels. As the earth brings forth its sprouts, and as a garden causes what is sown in it to sprout up, so cause righteousness and praise to sprout up before her. Amen (Isaiah 60 & 61).

*Even as the moon influences the tides of the sea, even so does prayer...influence the tides of godliness.* ~Charles Spurgeon

$\mathcal{A}$uthor of all existence,

For my wonderful wife's sake do not keep silent, and for her sake do not be quiet, until her righteousness goes forth as brightness, and her salvation as a burning torch. Let men see her righteousness, and women her glory, because You have called her by a new name that Your mouth has given. May she be as a crown of beauty in Your hand, and a royal diadem in the hand of her God. Let her be called My Delight Is in Her, for You delight in Your servant. Fill her with the joyful knowledge that You take pleasure in her, that as the bridegroom rejoices over the bride, so You rejoice over her. Please establish her and make her a praise in the earth. Let those who eat the grain and drink the wine of her house praise the LORD, and exult in Your holiness.

I beloved daughter of Zion, behold, your salvation has come; behold, His reward is Himself! Rejoice! For you are numbered among The Holy People, The Redeemed of the LORD; and you are called Sought Out, A Woman Not Forsaken.

O Mighty One, help her to put her hope in You—You who are splendid in Your apparel, marching in the greatness of Your strength, speaking in righteousness, mighty to save. Thank You for sparing her lifeblood and bringing to her salvation by Your powerful arm. Thank You, that when she deserved to be trod in Your anger and trampled in Your wrath, You gave Christ to bear her punishment! We bless His name together, for He is our joy and our salvation (Isaiah 62 & 63).

$\mathcal{S}$ource of all blessedness,

Let my wife be a woman who recounts Your steadfast love, Your praises, according to all that You have given us, and the great goodness to our house that You have granted us according to Your compassion, according to the abundance of Your steadfast love. Thank You for becoming her Savior; that in Your love and in Your pity You have redeemed her, and lifted her up and carried her. Please continue to lead her, to make for Yourself a glorious name.

O beloved, it is my joy once again to remind you that He is your Father, though Abraham does not know you; He, the LORD, is your Father, your Redeemer from of old is His name!

O LORD, do not make her wander from Your ways and harden her heart, so that she fears You not. Keep her, and let her wait for You. For from of old no one has heard or perceived by the ear, no eye has seen a God besides You, who acts for those who wait for Him. You meet her who joyfully works righteousness—her who remembers Your ways. Therefore may she present herself to You as a joyful servant of righteousness, remembering the ways of her God (Isaiah 63 & 64).

*If a man loves a woman as Christ loved the Church, he is going to do all in his power—he is even going to give his life—to see that she is made holy. He will be tender, but he will also be true. Love is not merely a gentle touch or a pat on the head. It is a refiner's fire. It burns to purify.* ~Elisabeth Elliot

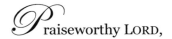 raiseworthy LORD,

I am glad and rejoice forever in my matchless wife whom You have created; for behold, You made her face to be my joy, and her presence to be my gladness. Give her the assurance that You also rejoice in her and are glad in Your people.

Let her live by faith, hoping for the day when You create a new heavens and a new earth—when the sound of weeping and the cry of distress shall be heard no more, when Your chosen shall not labor in vain or bear children for calamity, when the wolf and the lamb shall graze together.

Guard her from the subtle deceitfulness of pride; help her to fight against arrogance. For this is the one to whom You will look: she who is humble and contrite in spirit and trembles at Your word.

Let her see Your glory and declare it among the nations, so that all flesh may know that You are the LORD and come to worship before You (Isaiah 65 & 66).

*I*nfinitely worthy LORD,

I will sing to You, for You have done glorious things; You have made my most excellent wife, You made Yourself her strength and her song, and You have become her salvation! You are my God, and I will praise You for her; You are the God of Jacob, and I will exalt You. Your right hand, O LORD, glorious in power, Your right hand, O LORD, shatters her enemies. In the greatness of Your majesty You overthrow her adversaries; You send out Your fury; it consumes them like stubble.

Who is like You, O LORD, among the gods? Who is like You, majestic in holiness, awesome in glorious deeds, doing wonders? You have led in Your steadfast love my wife whom You have redeemed; You have guided her by Your strength to Your holy abode. You alone will reign forever and ever.

I will sing to You, for You have triumphed gloriously over her enemies; You will guard and defend her, for You have become her salvation! (Exodus 15).

*What is the reason that some believers are so much brighter and holier than others? I believe the difference, nineteen cases out of twenty, arises from different habits about private prayer. I believe that those who are not eminently holy pray little, and those who are eminently holy pray much. ~J. C. Ryle*

$\mathcal{M}$ost blessed LORD,

Let my wife be a woman who proclaims Your name and ascribes greatness to her God. For You are the Rock, whose work is perfect, for all Your ways are justice. A God of faithfulness and without iniquity, just and upright are You.

Keep her from becoming unmindful of the Rock that bore her, from forgetting the God who gave her birth. But make her remember and rejoice that You, even You, are her help, and there is no god beside You. You kill and You make alive; You wound and You heal; and there is none that can deliver out of Your hand.

Rejoice with Him, O beloved; bow down to Him, for He avenges the blood of His children and takes vengeance on His adversaries.

Most High God, let her dwell in safety; surround her all day long, and dwell between her shoulders. May she be blessed by You with favor, and be full of the blessing of the LORD. For there is none like You, who rides through the heavens to her help, through the skies in Your majesty. Be her dwelling place, and keep Your everlasting arms underneath her. Amen (Deuteronomy 32 & 33).

Lord GOD,

Who am I, and what is my house, that You have given me such a marvelous wife? And yet this was a small thing in Your eyes, O Lord GOD. According to Your own heart You have brought her to me, to make Your servant know Your abundant goodness. Therefore You are great, O LORD God. For there is none like You, and there is no God besides You.

And who is like my beautiful wife? I praise You that she is Your child, one of the women on earth whom You went to redeem to be Your daughter, making Yourself a name and doing for her great and awesome things. You established her for Yourself to be Yours forever. And You, O LORD, became her God.

And now, O LORD God, let Your name be magnified forever through her. Let her say, "The LORD of hosts is God over His people." Your promises are sure; You are her God, therefore Your servant has found courage to pray this prayer to You. May it please You to bless the wife of Your servant, so that she may continue forever before You. For only with Your blessing shall the wife of Your servant be blessed forever (II Samuel 7).

*The great fault of the children of God is, they do not continue in prayer; they do not go on praying; they do not persevere. If they desire anything for God's glory, they should pray until they get it. Oh, how good, and kind, and gracious, and condescending is the One with Whom we have to do! He has given me, unworthy as I am, immeasurably above all I had asked or thought!* ~George Mueller

$\mathcal{L}$ORD of Thunder,

Please be my dear wife's rock and her fortress and her deliverer, her God, her rock, in whom she takes refuge, her shield, and the horn of her salvation, her stronghold and her refuge, her savior; save her from violence. I call upon You, who are worthy to be praised, to plead for her perseverance.

When the waves of death encompass her, when the torrents of destruction assail her, let her hope in You. When the cords of Sheol entangle her, when the snares of death confront her, in her distress let her call upon You; may she call to her God. Hear her voice, and may her cry come to Your ears. Send from on high and take hold of her; draw her out of many waters. Rescue her and bring her out into a broad place; rescue her because You delight in her.

Enable her to keep Your ways and let her not wickedly depart from her God. May all Your rules be before her, and from Your statutes may she not turn aside. Make her blameless before You, and help her to keep herself from guilt. Mold her into a merciful, pure woman, for with the merciful You show Yourself merciful; with the blameless woman You show Yourself blameless; with the purified You deal purely, and with the crooked You make Yourself seem tortuous (II Samuel 22).

$\mathcal{S}$avior of a humble people,

Be my wife's lamp, O LORD, and lighten her darkness. Lead her in Your way, for Your way is perfect; Your word proves true; be a shield for her as she takes refuge in You. For who is God but You? And who is a rock, except You? Therefore please be her strong refuge and make her way blameless. Make her feet like the feet of a deer and set her securely on the heights. Train her hands for war, so that she may use the shield of Your salvation.

By Your gentleness make her great. Give a wide place for her steps under her, and let her feet not slip. Equip her with strength for battle; make the evil that rises against her sink under her.

O beloved, the LORD lives, and blessed be our rock, and exalted be our God, the rock of our salvation!

For this we will praise You, O LORD, among the nations, and sing praises to Your name! Bring great salvation to my wife, and show steadfast love to her forever (II Samuel 22).

*The prayerless spirit saps a people's moral strength because it blunts their thought and conviction of the Holy. It must be so if prayer is such a moral blessing and such a shaping power, if it pass, by its nature, from the vague volume and passion of devotion to formed petition and effort. Prayerlessness is an injustice and a damage to our own soul, and therefore to its history, both in what we do and what we think. The root of all deadly heresy is prayerlessness.* ~P. T. Forsyth

od of Jacob,

Raise up my marvelous wife to live in the fear of You, so that she may dawn on her children like the morning light, like the sun shining forth on a cloudless morning, like rain that makes grass to sprout from the earth.

Thank You that You have shown great and steadfast love to her, and have caused her to walk before You in faithfulness, in righteousness, and in uprightness of heart toward You. Please keep for her this great and steadfast love.

Give her an understanding mind that she may discern between good and evil. Grant her a wise and discerning mind, so that she may walk in Your ways, keeping Your statutes and Your commandments. For there is no God like You, O LORD, in heaven above or on earth beneath, keeping covenant and showing steadfast love to Your servants who walk before You with all their heart. Behold, heaven and the highest heaven cannot contain You, yet have regard to the prayer of Your servant and his plea, O LORD, my God, listening to the cry and to the prayer that Your servant prays before You this day on behalf of his wife. Let her fear You all the days that she lives, and may she shine forth the greatness of Your name, Your mighty hand, and Your outstretched arm (II Samuel 23, I Kings 3, 8).

*There are many good resources for learning how to pray, but the best way to learn how to pray is to pray.* ~Donald Whitney

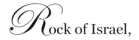ock of Israel,

There is no God like You, in heaven above or on earth beneath, keeping covenant and steadfast love to Your servants who walk before You with all their heart. Therefore I ask that You would incline the heart of my dearest wife to walk in Your ways, keeping Your statutes. Keep her in the way everlasting; let her pay close attention to her way, to walk before You as David walked before You. Listen to the plea of Your servant when I pray for her; hear from heaven and teach her the good way in which she should walk, and rain grace upon her that she may fear You all the days of her life.

Let Your eyes be open to her pleas, giving ear to her whenever she calls You. For You chose her from among all the people of the earth to be Your heritage.

Blessed are You, O LORD, who has given rest to my wife. Not one word has failed of all Your good promise, which You spoke to Moses Your servant, which is hers in Christ Jesus! Be with her, and do not leave her or forsake her, that You may incline her heart to Yourself, to walk in all Your ways and to keep Your commandments, Your statutes, and Your rules. Maintain her cause, that all the peoples of the earth may know that the LORD is God; there is no other. Let her heart therefore be wholly true to You our God, walking in Your statutes and keeping Your commandments (I Kings 8).

$\mathcal{O}$ LORD the God of Israel,

Who is enthroned above the cherubim,

You are the God, You alone, of all the kingdoms of the earth; You have made heaven and earth. Incline Your ear; O LORD, and hear; open Your eyes, O LORD, and see; and hear the words of my prayer on behalf of my glorious wife.

Let her give thanks to You; let her call upon Your name and make known Your deeds among the peoples! May she sing to You; let her sing praises to You and tell of all Your wonderful works! Cause her to glory in Your holy name; let her heart seek You and rejoice!

O beloved, chosen of Jacob, seek the LORD and His strength; seek His presence continually! Remember the wondrous works that He has done, His miracles and judgments He uttered.

LORD God, help her to remember Your covenant forever, the word that You commanded, for a thousand generations, the covenant that You made with Abraham. Let her sing to You with all the earth and tell of Your salvation from day to day! May she declare Your glory among the nations, Your marvelous works among all the peoples! For great are You, O LORD, and greatly to be praised, and You are to be held in awe above all gods. For all the gods of the peoples are idols, but You made the heavens. Splendor and majesty are before You; strength and joy are in Your place (II Kings 19 & I Chronicles 16).

$\mathcal{G}$od of my salvation,

Please increase my wife's desire to ascribe to You glory and strength—to ascribe to You the glory due Your name and come humbly before You! Let her worship You in the splendor of holiness, trembling before You with joy. Let her be glad with the heavens, and rejoice with the earth, and let her say among the nations, "The LORD reigns!" Let her roar with the sea, and all that fills it; let her exult with the field, and everything in it! Then make her sing for joy with the trees of the forest before You, for You come to judge the earth.

O beloved, give thanks to the LORD, for He is good; for His steadfast love endures forever.

Keep her to the end, O God of our salvation, and deliver her from among the nations, that she may give thanks to Your holy name, and glory in Your praise. For blessed are You, the God of Israel, from everlasting to everlasting! Amen. Praise the LORD! (I Chronicles 16).

*The opposite of planning is the rut. If you don't plan a vacation you will probably stay home and watch TV. The natural, unplanned flow of spiritual life sinks to the lowest ebb of vitality. There is a race to be run and a fight to be fought. If you want renewal in your life of prayer you must plan to see it.* ~John Piper.

$\mathcal{L}$ord of all being,

Let Your eyes be open and Your ears attentive to the prayer of Your servant. And now arise, O LORD, and go to her. Clothe her with salvation, and make her rejoice in Your goodness. O LORD God, do not turn away the face of Your anointed one! Remember Your steadfast love for my precious wife, Your servant. Let her worship You and give thanks to You, saying, "For He is good, for His steadfast love endures forever."

May she continually humble herself, and pray and seek Your face and turn from wicked ways. Open Your eyes and let Your ears be attentive to her, for You have chosen and consecrated her that Your name may be exalted forever. Let her praise You as the God of heaven, who rules over all the kingdoms of the nations—as the God in whose hand are power and might, so that none is able to withstand You. May she give thanks to You, for Your steadfast love endures forever (II Chronicles 6 & 20).

$\mathcal{M}$y God, the great, the mighty, and the awesome God,

O that my exquisite wife would delight herself in Your great goodness! Thank You that even when she forgets You and strays from Your commandments, in Your great mercies You do not make an end of her or forsake her, for You are a gracious and merciful God.

When hardships befall her, let them not seem little to You; when she cries to You hear from heaven and deliver her according to Your mercies.

Be exalted in Your grace, for although we have acted wickedly, You have dealt faithfully.

Let her not boast in her wisdom, nor in her might, nor in her riches, but let her boast in this: that she understands and knows You, that You are the LORD who practices steadfast love, and justice, and righteousness in the earth. For in these things You delight.

There is none like You, O LORD; You are great, and Your name is great in might. May she fear You, O King of the nations. For this is Your due; for among all the wise ones of the nations and in all their kingdoms there is none like You (Nehemiah 9, Jeremiah 9 & 10).

*As it is the business of tailors to make clothes and of cobblers to mend shoes, so it is the business of Christians to pray.* ~Martin Luther

ternal God,

Let my precious wife rejoice in the Word, through whom all things were made. May she seek life only in Him.

Praise be to Your name for causing her to receive Him and believe on His name, for giving her the right to become Your child. Open her eyes to the glory of the Word, the glory of Your only Son, full of grace and truth. From His fullness let her receive grace upon grace—the grace and truth that come through Jesus Christ. Help her to do what is true and come to the light, so that it may be clearly seen that her deeds have been carried out in You.

Help her not to judge by appearances, but instead to judge with right judgment. And when she thirsts, let her go to Christ and drink. Let her follow closely after Him always, so that she will not walk in darkness, but will have the light of life. Make her abide in His word as a true disciple so that she may know the truth and be set free by it (John 1 & 8).

*G*reat Life-Giver,

May my wonderful wife never faint in following after her Shepherd's voice. Let Christ go before her and lead her, calling her by name and wooing her with His words.

Let her flee from the stranger, from the thief, and from the robber, for she does not know their voice.

I praise You that she has entered by Your Son into salvation and plentiful pasture. May she have life and have it abundantly in Him, for that is why He came. Let her trust Him always as her good Shepherd who lays down His life for sheep like her.

Enable me to shepherd her as Christ does, to lay my own life down for her, to guard and guide her diligently. May I never be like the hired hand who sees the wolf coming and leaves her and flees.

O beloved, trust Christ as your Shepherd! For His Father, who has given you to Him, is greater than all, and no one is able to snatch you out of Your Father's hand. And Christ and the Father are one (John 10).

*Nothing would do more to cure us of a belief in our own wisdom than the granting of some of our eager prayers. And nothing could humiliate us more than to have God say when the fulfillment of our desire brought leanness to our souls, "Well, you would have it." It is what He has said to many. But He has said more, "My grace is sufficient for thee."*
~P. T. Forsyth

*A*lmighty Father,

Stir within my dear wife a stronger desire to glorify the Son of Man. Let her seek to glorify Him even in her death. For unless a grain of wheat falls into the earth and dies, it remains alone; but if it dies, it bears much fruit. And my desire is that she bear much fruit for the splendor of Your name. Therefore let her not love her life and so lose it, but help her to hate her life in this world so that she may keep it for eternal life. May she serve Christ and follow Christ, for then You will honor her.

Even in this very hour, Father, glorify Your name in her. Draw her to Yourself and let Christ always be her light, that she may not walk in darkness. Thank You that she has believed in the light and has become a daughter of light. I praise You that You did not blind her eyes or harden her heart so that she could not believe. But in grace You shone into her soul and made her to love the glory that comes from You more than the glory that comes from man (John 12).

$\mathcal{F}$ather of our Lord and Teacher,

Help my lovely wife and me to persevere in washing one another's feet in all humility and joy. For Christ has given us an example, that we should also do as He has done to us. Assist us to do what we know as servants, for a servant is not greater than his master.

Please deliver my wife from the treachery that still indwells her, for if You remove Your hand of grace she will surely betray Your Son. O spare her that dreadful end! Keep her faithful and steadfast in Jesus all her days, so that He may be glorified, and You will be glorified in Him.

Cause us to grow in love for one another—to strive wholeheartedly to love each other just as Christ has loved us, so that all people will know that we are His disciples, if we have love for one another.

O beloved, let not your heart be troubled! Believe in God; believe also in Christ.

Father, fill her afresh with hope for the time when Your Son will come again and will take her to Himself, that where He is she may be also (John 13 & 14).

*Prayer is a special exercise of faith. Faith makes the prayer acceptable because it believes that either the prayer will be answered, or that something better will be given instead.* ~Martin Luther

*Author of Pleasure,*

All thanks and praise belong to You for showing my winsome wife the way to Yourself, which is through Jesus alone. Blessed be Your glorious name for revealing Christ to her as the way, and the truth, and the life! May she grow to know Him better today than she did yesterday, which is to know You, His Father. I ask this only in Your Son's name, that You may be glorified in Him.

Create within her deeper love for Christ, and let this love constrain her to keep His commandments. Thank You for giving her another Helper to be with her forever, even the Spirit of truth, whom the world cannot receive, because it neither sees Him nor knows Him. Let her sing praise to You, for Your Spirit dwells in her.

O beloved, do not despair, for Christ has not left us as orphans; He will come to us.

Father, may she love Christ and keep His words. By Your Holy Spirit, teach her all things and bring to her remembrance all that Christ has spoken. Grant His peace to her. Amen (John 14).

*S*overeign Vinedresser,

Let not my precious wife's heart be troubled, neither let it be afraid. Remind her that Christ is mighty to save, and You will not leave her or forsake her. Help her to do as You have commanded her, so that the world may know that she loves You.

Please make her a branch that bears fruit because she abides in the vine, which is Christ. Prune her, that she may bear more fruit. Preserve her as one who abides in Christ and He in her, so that she bears much fruit, for apart from Christ she can do nothing.

O beloved, let us abide always in Jesus, with His words abiding in us. For then, when we ask whatever we wish, it will be done for us.

Father, glorify Yourself by making her bear much fruit, and so proving her to be Christ's disciple. May she abide in His love, for as You have loved Him, so has He loved her. Cause her to keep His commandments, for then she will abide in His love, just as He abides in Your love by keeping Your commandments.

Come quickly, Lord Jesus. Amen (John 14 & 15).

*Humbly I asked of God to give me joy,*
*To crown my life with blossoms of delight;*
*I pled for happiness without alloy,*
*Desiring that my pathway should be bright;*
*Prayerfully I sought these blessings to attain, —*
*And now I thank him that he gave me pain....*

*For with the pain and sorrow came to me*
*A dower of tenderness in act and thought;*
*And with the failure came a sympathy,*
*An insight that success had never bought.*
*Father, I had been foolish and unblest*
*If thou had granted me my blind request!*

~L. M. Montgomery

lecting God,

Thank You for choosing my lovely wife and appointing her that she should go and bear fruit and that her fruit should abide. How gracious You are to call her Your friend! Fill her with love for her brothers and sisters in Christ, and for me. And fill me with fresh, fervent, bright, divinely-wrought love for her.

If the world hates her, remind her that it hated Christ before it hated her. Prepare her to expect the world's hatred, for You chose her out of the world and she is no longer of the world. Help her to remember the word spoken by Christ: "A servant is not greater than his master," so that she will not be surprised or lose heart when persecution comes.

Let her persevere in bearing witness about Your glorious Son and enable her to do so by Your wonderful Helper, the Spirit of truth, who proceeds from You. May she herald the name of Jesus with boldness and joy.

In the midst of persecution, Father, keep her from falling away! May her heart not falter in unbelief (John 15).

$\mathcal{M}$agnificent Father,

Now that Your Spirit of truth has come, let Him guide my marvelous wife into all the truth. May He glorify the Son by taking what is Christ's and declaring it to her. When she is sorrowful, turn her sorrow into joy. Fill her with hope that she will see Christ again soon, and then her heart will rejoice and no one will take her joy from her. Give her confidence to ask things of You in the name of Christ, for then she will receive, that her joy may be full. Imbue her soul with joy in Jesus! Cause her to listen to His words, that in Him she may have peace.

O beloved, in the world you will have tribulation. But take heart; Christ has overcome the world!

Father, grant her to know You, the only true God, and Jesus Christ more deeply, for that is eternal life. Enable her to glorify You on earth and accomplish the work that You have given her to do. Holy Father, keep us in Your name, that we may be one, even as You and Christ are one. Guard her so that she may never be lost. Open her ears to the words spoken by Your Son that she may have His joy fulfilled in herself. Thank You for giving us Your word through Christ! Amen (John 16 & 17).

*O what peace we often forfeit,*
*O what needless pain we bear,*
*All because we do not carry*
*Everything to God in prayer!*
~Joseph Scriven

$\mathcal{G}$od and Father of my Lord Jesus Christ,

Praise be to Your name because You have blessed my dear wife in Christ with every spiritual blessing in the heavenly places, even as You chose her in Him before the foundation of the world, that she should be holy and blameless before You. Please continue to sanctify her by the love with which You predestined her for adoption through Jesus Christ, according to the purpose of Your will, to the praise of Your glorious grace, with which You have blessed her in the Beloved. Worthy is He! How beautiful is Your Son! Let His name be exalted! For in Him she has redemption through His blood, the forgiveness of her trespasses, according to the riches of Your grace, which You lavished on her, in all wisdom and insight.

O beloved, let us laud His name together for His rich and lavish grace toward us! For in Christ we have obtained an inheritance, having been predestined according to the purpose of Him who works all things according to the counsel of His will, so that we who hope in Christ might be to the praise of His glory!

Father, remind her of her former state as a child of wrath by nature, like the rest of mankind, when she was dead in her trespasses and sins. Remind her of this so that she will rejoice afresh that You, being rich in mercy, because of the great love with which You loved her, even when she was dead in her trespasses, made her alive with Christ and saved her by grace. Continue showing her the immeasurable riches of Your grace in kindness toward her in Christ Jesus. Amen (Ephesians 1 & 2).

$\mathcal{M}$ighty God,

Thank You for saving my resplendent wife by pure grace, so that she cannot boast as if it were her own doing, for her salvation is a gift of You and not a result of works. I praise Your name alone for the inestimable treasure that I have in her, because she is Your workmanship, created in Christ Jesus for good works. Therefore assist her to walk in the good works which You prepared beforehand for her.

Remind her constantly that she was at one time separated from Christ, having no hope and without God in the world. Remind her, so that she may rejoice continually that now in Christ Jesus she has been brought near by His blood. Fill her with the confidence that comes from knowing that Christ Himself is her peace—that He has reconciled her to You through the cross. Let her sing for joy anew because He has broken down the dividing wall of hostility between her and You—the one true and holy God.

In Christ please continue building us together into a dwelling place for Yourself by the Spirit. Amen (Ephesians 2).

*No tongue can express, no mind can reach, the heavenly placidness and soul-satisfying delight which are intimated in these words [Eph 2:18]. To come to God as a Father, through Christ, by the help and assistance of the Holy Spirit, revealing him as a Father unto us, and enabling us to go to him as a Father, how full of sweetness and satisfaction is it!*
~John Bunyan

$\mathcal{G}$od of revealed mystery,

O that my remarkable wife would be granted insight into the mystery of Christ by Your Spirit! Give her more and more depth of understanding of this marvelous mystery—that in Christ, through the gospel, she is a fellow heir with the commonwealth of Israel, a member of His body, and a partaker of the promise. By the working of Your power give her much grace to minister to those in need. Grant her more grace to love and spread the unsearchable riches of Christ, and to bring to light for many what is the plan of the mystery hidden for ages in You who created all things. Through her make known Your manifold wisdom.

Empower her to walk in a manner worthy of the calling to which she has been called, with all humility and gentleness, with patience, bearing with others in love, eager to maintain the unity of the Spirit in the bond of peace. Keep enlarging her heart and mind with the knowledge of Your Son, unto mature womanhood, to the measure of the stature of the fullness of Christ, so that she may not be a child, tossed to and fro by the waves and carried about by every wind of doctrine. Guard her from human cunning, from craftiness in deceitful schemes. Enable her to speak the truth in love, to grow up in every way into Him who is the head, into Christ, and to work properly as a member of His body, helping to build it up in love (Ephesians 2 & 3).

Condescending God,

Prevent my wonderful wife from walking as the world does, in the futility of their minds. Do not let her live as one darkened in her understanding, hard of heart, callous, or greedy to practice every kind of impurity.

Instead, help her to put off her old self, which is corrupt through deceitful desires. Renew her in the spirit of her mind, and empower her to put on the new self, created after Your likeness in true righteousness and holiness. Make her put away falsehood and speak the truth with her neighbor.

When she is angry keep her from sin; grant her the grace to not let the sun go down on her anger. Let no corrupting talk come out of her mouth, but only such as is good for building up, as fits the occasion, that it may give grace to those who hear. And let her not grieve Your Holy Spirit, by whom she was sealed for the day of redemption. Put all bitterness and wrath and anger and clamor and slander away from her, along with all malice.

Grow us in kindness toward one another, make us tenderhearted, so that we may be always forgiving each other as You forgave us in Christ. Amen (Ephesians 4).

*The first reason why prayer leads to fullness of joy is that prayer is the nerve center of our fellowship with Jesus. He is not here physically to see. But in prayer we speak to Him just as though He were. And in the stillness of those sacred times, we listen to His Word and we pour out to Him our longings.* ~John Piper

*F*ather of glory,

Assist my lovely wife to be an imitator of You, as Your beloved daughter. And make her walk in love, as Christ loved us and gave Himself up for us, a fragrant offering and sacrifice to You.

Keep her from any form or appearance of sexual immorality and all impurity or covetousness. And let us both guard our tongues, so that there might not be any filthiness or foolish talk or crude joking, which are out of place, but instead make us abound with thanksgiving.

Guide her feet to walk as a child of light, and enable her to discern what is pleasing to You. Let her take no part in the unfruitful works of darkness, but instead expose them. Open her eyes to look carefully how she walks, not as unwise but as wise, making the best use of the time, because the days are evil. Therefore help her to understand what Your will is.

Fill us with Your Spirit so that we may address one another in psalms and hymns and spiritual songs, singing and making melody to You with all of our heart, giving thanks always and for everything to You in the name of our Lord Jesus Christ. And it is in His name that I come to You with this plea for grace. Amen (Ephesians 5).

$\mathcal{S}$overeign LORD,

Shall we receive good from You, and shall we not receive evil? Therefore may my precious wife hold fast to her integrity when calamity comes. Instead of cursing, let her bless You saying, "The LORD gave, and the LORD has taken away; blessed be the name of the LORD." When evil befalls her, let her not charge You with wrong or sin with her lips. And when her suffering is great, enable me to comfort her in wisdom and in righteousness.

May she seek You, and to You may she commit her cause. For You do great things and unsearchable, marvelous things without number: You set on high those who are lowly, and those who mourn are lifted up to safety. You save the needy from the sword of the mouth of the crafty and from the hand of the mighty.

Beloved, behold, your God is faithful when He wounds and shatters you even in your blamelessness. Therefore, do not despise His hard hand of grace, for He binds up, and His hands heal.

Father, deliver my wife from troubles! In famine redeem her from death, and in war from the power of the sword! Hide her from the lash of the tongue, and let her not fear destruction when it comes! (Job 1, 2, 4, 5).

*As prayer without faith is but a beating of the air, so trust without prayers [is] but a presumptuous bravado. He that promises to give, and bids us trust his promises, commands us to pray, and expects obedience to his commands. He will give, but not without our asking.*
~Thomas Lye

## Merciful Almighty,

I am but of yesterday and know nothing, for my days on earth are a shadow. Therefore give wisdom to your servant and deal kindly with me that I might live uprightly with the precious woman You have made for me. Please fill her mouth with laughter, and her lips with shouting. Let those who hate her be clothed with shame, for You are wise in heart and mighty in strength. You command the sun, and it does not rise; You seal up the stars; You alone stretched out the heavens and trampled the waves of the sea; You made the Bear and Orion, the Pleiades and the chambers of the south; You do great things beyond searching out, and marvelous things beyond number.

O how greatly and marvelously You have made my wife! And what a great marvel that You have saved her and kept her with the strength of Your right hand! Praise and glory are due Your name, for You have provided an arbiter between her and Yourself, even the man Jesus Christ, so that You have taken Your rod away from her, and Your dread no longer terrifies her. Therefore may she never loathe her life, or speak in bitterness of soul, for behold, she has an advocate with You, Jesus Christ the righteous (Job 8, 9, 10, I John 2).

*H*elper of the weak,

I give You praise and thanks for my wife, so matchless in beauty and integrity of heart. For Your hands fashioned and made her. You clothed her with skin and flesh, and knit her together with bones and sinews. You have granted her life and steadfast love, and Your care has preserved her spirit.

Therefore please do not destroy her altogether. Remember that You have made her like clay, and do not return her to the dust. Are not her days few? Therefore please bless her, and do not fill her with disgrace. Work wonders *for* her, and not against her.

Oh, that You would speak and open Your lips to her, and that You would tell her the secrets of wisdom! For You are manifold in understanding.

Know, beloved, that God exacts of you less than your guilt deserves, because of Christ. He has taken your guilt upon Himself, therefore be of good cheer and rejoice in the abundant life given you in Him!

Thank You, Father, that because of Your Son, she can lift up her face without blemish; she can be secure and not fear. Let her life be brighter than the noonday, and its darkness like the morning. May she feel secure, because there is hope—hope in Jesus. Let her lie down with none to make her afraid. Amen (Job 10 & 11).

*Prayer is the most tangible expression of trust in God.* ~Jerry Bridges

$\mathcal{G}$reat God,

In whose hand is the life of every living thing and the breath of all mankind, with You are wisdom and might; You have counsel and understanding. Therefore, impart these things to my magnificent wife. Lead her with strength and sound wisdom. Let the eyes of her heart feast upon Your splendor. Let them brighten at the sight of Your justice, and with the vision of Your righteousness. For You overthrow the mighty. You uncover the deeps out of darkness and bring deep darkness to light. You make nations great, and You destroy them; You enlarge nations, and lead them away.

When Your majesty terrifies her, and the dread of You falls upon her, let her run to Christ. Even when I am a worthless physician in the day of her calamity, let her cling continually to Christ. And though You slay her, let her hope in You. Do not hide Your face or count her as Your enemy. Please do not frighten her or make her inherit the iniquities of her youth (Job 12 & 13).

*Prayer is the acknowledgment of God's sovereignty and of our dependence upon Him to act on our behalf. Prudence is the acknowledgment of our responsibility to use all legitimate means. We must not separate the two.* ~Jerry Bridges

𝓜ajestic and mighty LORD,

Make my wife wise. Impart to her holy insight. And let her not do away with the fear of God, or hinder meditation before You. Keep her iniquity from teaching her mouth, and let her not choose the tongue of the crafty. Open her ears to listen to Your council, so that she does not limit wisdom to herself.

Protect her from the one who is abominable and corrupt, the man who drinks injustice like water. Let not distress and anguish terrify her; may they not prevail against her, for she has not trusted in emptiness, deceiving herself. Do not tear her with Your wrath or hate her, or gnash Your teeth at her. Neither give her up to the ungodly or cast her into the hands of the wicked. Please do not break her apart, or seize her by the neck and dash her to pieces, or set her up as Your target, surrounding her with Your archers. Do not break her with breach upon breach, or run upon her like a warrior. For even though she deserves all these things, spare her because of Christ, for she abides in Him.

O beloved, hope continually in Christ! Look to Him alone for your salvation. Even now, behold, your witness is in heaven, and He who testifies for you is on high. He argues your case with God, as a son of man does with his neighbor.

O Father we offer You praise and thanks for the advocate You have given us in Jesus! (Job 15 & 16).

$\mathcal{R}$estorer of the broken in spirit,

Even when my beautiful wife makes her bed in darkness, when reproach is cast upon her, when You strip her glory from her, and set darkness upon her paths, when her relatives fail her, and close friends forget her, when her intimate friends abhor her and those whom she loves turn against her, let her hope in Christ. For He lives, and has stood upon the earth, and she shall see Him for herself. Her eyes shall behold Him! May she long for that day and not lose heart.

Because she is found in Christ, let her children dance. Let them sing to the tambourine and the lyre and rejoice to the sound of the pipe. May they spend their days in prosperity. Let her receive instruction from Your Son's mouth, and lay up His words in her heart. Cause her to turn always to You so that she will be built up, and remove injustice far from her house.

O beloved, if you lay gold in the dust, and gold of Ophir among the stones of the torrent bed, then the Almighty will be your gold and your precious silver. For then you will delight yourself in the Almighty and lift up your face to God.

When she prays to You, hear her, and make light to shine on her ways. Be exalted! For You deliver her even though she is not innocent, and will grant her cleanness of hands (Job 17, 19, 21, 22).

*Whether we like it or not, asking is the rule of the Kingdom.*
~Charles Spurgeon

**R**ighteous Judge,

Thank You that Christ comes even to Your seat and lays the case of my wife before You. He alone is the upright man who can argue on her behalf so that she is acquitted forever by her Judge.

Behold, You know the way that she takes; when You have tried her, let her come out as gold. Make her foot hold fast to Your steps; keep her in Your way and do not let her turn aside. Let her never depart from the commandment of Your lips; may she treasure the words of Your mouth more than her portion of food.

You are unchangeable, and who can turn You back? What You desire, do so in her. Complete what You have appointed for her. Even if You must terrify her and make her heart faint, let her hope in Your steadfast love. May she trust Your hand when thick darkness covers her face. Amen (Job 23).

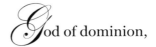od of dominion,

Is there any number to Your armies? Upon whom does Your light not arise? Thank You, that because of Christ, my dear wife is in the right before You. Be praised! For she who is born of woman has Him as her purity. His hand pierced the fleeing serpent, and by His spirit she has been made fair.

O beloved, adore and fear our God with me. He stretches out the north over the void and hangs the earth on nothing. The pillars of heaven tremble and are astounded at His rebuke. By His power He stilled the sea; by His understanding He shattered Rahab, the terror of the deep. Behold, these are but the outskirts of His ways, and how small a whisper do we hear of Him!

Father, as long as her breath is in her, and Your spirit is in her nostrils, keep her lips from speaking falsehood, and her tongue from uttering deceit. Let her hold fast to Christ's righteousness and not let it go.

Grant her wisdom. For You alone understand the way to it, and know its place. You said, "Behold, the fear of the Lord, that is wisdom, and to turn away from evil is understanding." Therefore increase her fear of You; let her turn away from evil and gain a discerning heart (Job 25-28).

$\mathcal{W}$ise Almighty,

Oh, that You might watch over my comely wife, making Your lamp to shine upon her head, so that by Your light she may walk through darkness. Let Your friendship be upon our house, and stay always with her.

Keep her children all around her; may her steps be washed with blessing, and cause the rock to pour out for her streams of oil. When the ear hears of her, let it call her blessed, and when the eye sees her, let it approve, because she delivers the poor who cry for help, and the fatherless who have none to help them.

May the blessings of those who are about to perish come upon her, and may she cause the widow's heart to sing for joy. Put righteousness on her and clothe her with it; make her justice like a robe and a turban.

Let her be eyes to the blind, feet to the lame, and mother to the needy. Let her search out the cause of even the one whom she does not know. Use her to break the fangs of the unrighteous and make them drop their prey from their teeth (Job 29).

*An attitude of acceptance says that we trust God, that He loves us, and knows what is best for us. Acceptance does not mean that we do not pray for physical healing, or for the conception and birth of a little one to our marriage. We should indeed pray for those things, but we should pray in a trusting way. We should realize that, though God can do all things, for infinitely wise and loving reasons, He may not do that which we pray that He will do. How do we know how long to pray? As long as we can pray trustingly, with an attitude of acceptance of His will, we should pray as long as the desire remains.* ~Jerry Bridges

$\mathcal{G}$od of justice and righteousness,

Make my dear wife wise. Fill her with understanding so that women will listen to her and wait and keep silence for her counsel—that they may wait for her as for the rain and open their mouths as for the spring rain.

Let her not despair when her soul is poured out within her, when days of affliction have taken hold of her. When she is cast into the mire, and has become like dust and ashes, let her cry to You for help, and answer her. Even when You seem to have turned cruel to her, may she hope in Your promise; may she wait for Your unfailing love. Let her be a woman who weeps for those whose days are hard, and whose soul grieves for the needy.

Assist me to comfort her when evil comes; when she has waited for light, but darkness comes. Grant me wisdom and compassion to bear her turmoil with her; to encourage her when days of affliction come to meet her. Be merciful to her, for she has not walked with falsehood and her foot has not hastened to deceit (Job 30).

$\mathcal{M}$ajestic LORD,

Keep my marvelous wife from making gold her trust or calling fine gold her confidence. Let her not rejoice only because her wealth is abundant or because her hand has found much. Guard her heart from being secretly enticed to worship the shining splendor of what has been made, for that would be false to You. May she not rejoice at the ruin of the one who hates her, or exult when evil overtakes him. Let not her mouth sin by asking for his life with a curse.

Sanctify her so that she may be able to say that the sojourner has not lodged in the street, that she has opened her doors to the traveler, that she has withheld nothing that the poor desired, and has not caused the eyes of the widow to fail, that she has not left the fatherless hungry. Keep her from concealing her transgressions as others do by hiding iniquity in her bosom.

O beloved, behold, I am toward God as you are; I too was pinched off from a piece of clay. Let us together cling to Christ as our righteousness, for He is pure, without transgression; He is clean, and there is no iniquity in Him (Job 31 & 33).

*Intercessory prayer is the purifying bath into which the individual and the fellowship must enter every day.* ~Dietrich Bonhoeffer

$\mathcal{O}$God, who is greater than man,

Let my wife hope in Christ when her soul draws near the pit, and her life to those who bring death. May her flesh become fresh with youth; let her return to the days of her youthful vigor. When she prays to You, please accept her; may she see Your face with a shout of joy, as You restore to her her righteousness.

O beloved, sing with me before men and say, "I sinned and perverted what was right, and it was not repaid to me. The LORD has redeemed my soul from going down into the pit, and my life shall look upon the light."

Do all these things with her, O Father, to bring back her soul from the pit, that she may be lighted with the light of life.

Listen to me; hear my words and give ear to me. Please teach my wife wisdom. Thank You that she does not drink up scoffing like water, that You have kept her from being a woman who travels in company with evildoers or walks with wicked men. May she never say, "It profits a woman nothing that she should take delight in God," for such are the words of the wicked (Job 33 & 34).

*True, whole prayer is nothing but love.* ~St. Augustine

$\mathcal{O}$Father, perfect in knowledge,

Be praised among the nations! For You have made my priceless wife because You are mighty in strength and understanding. Do not despise her; when she is afflicted please give her her right and keep her alive. Do not withdraw Your eyes from her.

Open her ears to instruction and help her to return from iniquity. May she listen and serve You, and complete her days in prosperity, and her years in pleasantness. Let her not cherish anger as the godless in heart. Deliver her by her affliction and open her ear by adversity. Allure her out of distress into a broad place, and may what is set on her table be full of fatness.

O beloved, behold, God is exalted in His power; who is a teacher like Him? Who has prescribed for Him His way, or who can say, "You have done wrong?" Remember to extol His work, of which men have sung. Behold, God is great, and we know Him not, the number of His years is unsearchable. For He draws up the drops of water; they distill His mist in rain which the skies pour down and drop on mankind abundantly. Can anyone understand the spreading of the clouds, the thunderings of His pavilion? Behold, He scatters His lightning about Him and covers the roots of the sea. For by these He judges peoples; He gives food in abundance. He covers His hands with the lightning and commands it to strike the mark. Its crashing declares His presence; the cattle also declare that He rises (Job 36).

*G*od of thunderous majesty,

Let my lovely wife sing of Your power; when she sees it let her heart tremble and leap out of its place. For You thunder wondrously with Your voice; You do great things that we cannot comprehend. May she bow before You when she beholds the strength of Your word, for to the snow You say, "Fall on the earth," likewise to the downpour, Your mighty downpour. May she worship You with a reverent heart, for by Your breath ice is given, and the broad waters are frozen fast. Let her heart tremble before You in wonder, for You load the thick cloud with moisture; the clouds scatter Your lightning. They turn around and around by Your guidance, to accomplish all that You command them on the face of the habitable world. Whether for correction or for Your land or for love, You cause it to happen.

Hear me, O beloved; stop and consider the wondrous works of God.

LORD, I praise You, for she indeed is one of Your most wondrous works—more amazing than the rain, the lightning, the wind, or the clouds; she shines and declares the glory of Him who is perfect in knowledge.

May she worship You as she looks on the light when it is bright in the skies, when the wind has passed and cleared them. Out of the north comes golden splendor; You are clothed with awesome majesty. Let her praise You as the One great in power, in justice, and abundant in righteousness. Therefore, let her fear You. Amen (Job 37).

$\mathcal{F}$ather of my Lord Jesus Christ,

According to Your foreknowledge, in the sanctification of the Spirit, for obedience to Jesus Christ and for sprinkling with His blood: may grace and peace be multiplied to my wonderful wife.

Let her bless You, for according to Your great mercy, You have caused her to be born again to a living hope through the resurrection of Jesus Christ from the dead, to an inheritance that is imperishable, undefiled, and unfading, kept in heaven for her. Thank You that by Your power she is being guarded through faith for a salvation ready to be revealed in the last time. Let her rejoice in this. May she rejoice even when it is necessary that she be grieved for a little while by various trials, so that the tested genuineness of her faith—more precious than gold that perishes though it is tested by fire—may be found to result in praise and glory and honor at the revelation of Jesus Christ. Though she has not seen Him, let her love Him all the more. Though she does not now see Him, I praise You that she believes in Him and rejoices with joy that is inexpressible and filled with glory, obtaining the outcome of her faith, the salvation of her soul (I Peter 1).

*Prayer does not fit us for the greater work, prayer is the greater work.*
~Oswald Chambers

$\mathcal{F}$ather of our living hope,

O that You would assist my exquisite wife to prepare her mind for action, and to be sober-minded. Let her set her hope fully on the grace that will be brought to her at the revelation of Jesus Christ. As an obedient child, may she not be conformed to the passions of her former ignorance. Instead, as You who called her are holy, make her holy in all her conduct, since it is written, "You shall be holy, for I am holy." And since You are her Father who judges impartially according to her deeds, cause her to conduct herself with fear throughout the time of her exile on this earth, knowing that she was ransomed from the futile ways inherited from her forefathers, not with perishable things such as silver or gold, but with the precious blood of Christ, like that of a lamb without blemish or spot.

O beloved, He was made manifest in the last times for your sake, for through Him you are a believer in God, who raised Him from the dead and gave Him glory, so that your faith and hope are in God.

Enable us, O LORD, to purify our souls by our obedience to the truth for a sincere love, so that we may love one another earnestly from a pure heart, since we have been born again, not of perishable seed but of imperishable, through Your living and abiding word. Praise be to Your name! For this word is the good news that was preached to us. Amen (I Peter 1).

ternal LORD,

By Your mighty Spirit enable my wife to put away all malice and all deceit and hypocrisy and envy and all slander. Make her long for the pure spiritual milk, that by it she may grow up to salvation—since indeed she has tasted that You are good.

Thank You that as she comes to Christ, a living stone rejected by men but in Your sight chosen and precious, she is being built up like a living stone into a spiritual house to be part of a holy priesthood, to offer spiritual sacrifices acceptable to You through Jesus Christ.

I praise You that she is part of Your chosen race, Your royal priesthood, Your holy nation, and a people for Your own possession. And because she is, let her ever proclaim Your excellencies—for You are the God who has called her out of darkness into Your marvelous light. Thank You that although she once was not of a people, now she is of Your people; once she had not received mercy, but now she has received mercy.

Beloved, I urge you as a sojourner and exile to abstain from the passions of the flesh, which wage war against your soul.

Father, keep her conduct among the Gentiles honorable, so that when they speak against her as an evildoer, they may see her good deeds and glorify You on the day of visitation (I Peter 2).

*To clasp the hands in prayer is the beginning of an uprising against the disorder of the world.* ~Karl Barth

$\mathcal{L}$ORD of unbounded mercy,

Help my pure wife to live as one who is free, not using her freedom as a cover-up for evil, but living as Your bondservant. Let her honor everyone, love the brotherhood, fear You, and honor the governing authorities.

Grant her the grace to endure sorrows while suffering unjustly, being mindful of You. For if when she does good and suffers for it she endures, this is a gracious thing in Your sight.

For to this you have been called, my beloved, because Christ also suffered for you leaving an example, so that you might follow in His steps. He committed no sin, neither was deceit found in His mouth.

O God, make her like Him, so that when she is reviled, she will not revile in return. When she suffers, let her not threaten, but continue entrusting herself to You who judge justly. Thank You that we have a perfect example in Christ Jesus! He himself bore our sins in His body on the tree, that we might die to sin and live to righteousness. May He be exalted! For by His wounds we have been healed. Thank You, that even though she was straying like a sheep, now she has returned to You, the Shepherd and Overseer of her soul. Amen (I Peter 2).

*Y*ou who have called us to Your eternal glory in Christ,

Help me to live with my lovely wife in an understanding way, showing honor to her as the weaker vessel, since she is an heir with me of the grace of life. Help me to do this so that my prayers may not be hindered.

Do not let her repay evil for evil or reviling for reviling, but on the contrary, may she bless, for to this she was called, that she may obtain a blessing. I desire her to love life and see good days, therefore keep her tongue from evil and her lips from speaking deceit; let her turn away from evil and do good; let her seek peace and pursue it. For Your eyes are on the righteous, and Your ears are open to their prayer. But Your face is against those who do evil.

O beloved, even if you should suffer for righteousness' sake, you will be blessed. Rejoice, and have no fear of man, nor be troubled.

Father, may she regard Christ the Lord as holy in her heart, and always be prepared to make a defense to anyone who asks her for a reason for the hope that is in her. Let her do it with gentleness and respect, having a good conscience, so that, when she is slandered, those who revile her good behavior in Christ may be put to shame (I Peter 3).

*God delights in the aroma of his own glory*
*as he smells it in the prayers of his people.* ~John Piper

*G*od of all Grace,

If my courageous wife is insulted for the name of Christ, let her take comfort in the truth that she is blessed, because the Spirit of glory and of God rests upon her. If she suffers as a Christian, let her not be ashamed, but let her glorify You in that name. Indeed, when she suffers according to Your will, let her entrust her soul to You—her faithful Creator—while doing good.

Beloved, do not be surprised at the fiery trial when it comes upon you to test you, as though something strange were happening to you. But rejoice insofar as you share Christ's sufferings, that you may also rejoice and be glad when His glory is revealed.

Father, help me to shepherd this priceless woman with whom You have entrusted me, not under compulsion, but eagerly and joyfully, as You would have me; not domineering over her, but being an example. Please clothe us both with humility toward one another, for You oppose the proud but give grace to the humble. We want *You*. We need Your grace. Humble us, therefore, under Your mighty hand so that at the proper time You may exalt us. We cast our anxieties on You, because You care for us. Make us sober-minded. May we be watchful. Enable us to resist our adversary the devil firm in our faith, and remind us that the same kinds of suffering are being experienced by our brotherhood throughout the world. And when we have suffered a little while, restore, confirm, strengthen, and establish us. To You be the dominion forever and ever. Amen (I Peter 4 & 5).

$\mathcal{C}$ompassionate Father,

May grace and peace be multiplied to my incomparable wife in the knowledge of You and of Jesus our Lord. Thank You that Your divine power has granted to her all things that pertain to life and godliness, through the knowledge of You who called us to Your own glory and excellence, by which You have granted to her Your precious and very great promises, so that through them she may become a partaker of the divine nature, having escaped from the corruption that is in the world because of sinful desire.

Because of this great blessing, help her to make every effort to supplement her faith with virtue, and virtue with knowledge, and knowledge with self-control, and self-control with steadfastness, and steadfastness with godliness, and godliness with sisterly affection, and sisterly affection with love. Make these qualities her own and let them increase in her, to keep her from being ineffective or unfruitful in the knowledge of our Lord Jesus Christ. May she never be so nearsighted that she is blind, forgetting that she was cleansed from her former sins. Therefore, assist her to be all the more diligent to make her calling and election sure, for if she practices these qualities she will never fall. Please uphold her! And richly provide for her an entrance into the eternal kingdom of our Lord and Savior Jesus Christ. Hasten the coming of His kingdom, I pray. Amen (II Peter 1).

*Prayer is the power that wields the weapon of the Word;*
*but the Word itself is the weapon by which the nations*
*will be brought to faith and obedience.* ~John Piper

$\mathcal{F}$aithful King,

Make my wife the sort of woman who lives a life of holiness and godliness, waiting for and hastening the coming of the day of God, because of which the heavens will be set on fire and dissolved, and the heavenly bodies will melt as they burn. While we wait for a new heavens and a new earth in which righteousness dwells, let her be diligent to be found by You without spot or blemish, and at peace.

Protect her from false teachers that will rise up and secretly bring destructive heresies. Let her not be found among the many who will follow their sensuality and blaspheme the way of truth. Keep her far from the way of the unrighteous, who speak loud boasts of folly and are slaves to corruption. May it never be that after she has escaped the defilements of the world through the knowledge of our Lord and Savior Jesus Christ, she is again entangled in them and overcome! Guard her from such a fate, for her last state would become worse for her than the first.

Therefore, beloved, take care that you are not carried away with the error of lawless people and lose your own stability. But grow in the grace and knowledge of our Lord and Savior Jesus Christ.

Father, may she grow in such grace and knowledge! To You be the glory both now and to the day of eternity. Amen (II Peter 2 & 3).

Father,

Let whatever happens to my elegant wife serve to advance the gospel, so that even her suffering and imprisonment may magnify Christ. May her life be a source of confidence for others in You, that makes them much more bold to speak the word without fear.

Keep her from proclaiming Christ out of envy or rivalry, and instead let her do so from good will and out of love. More than that, let her rejoice in Christ, and in His truth proclaimed. And help her to continue stirring up others for their progress and joy in the faith.

Please let her manner of life be worthy of the gospel of Christ, so that we may stand firm in one spirit, with one mind striving side by side for the faith of the gospel, and not frightened in anything by our opponents. Thank you that it has been granted to us that for the sake of Christ we should not only believe in Him but also suffer for His sake.

Fill us with the joy of being of the same mind, having the same love, being in full accord and of one mind. Keep us from doing anything from rivalry or conceit, but let us in humility count others more significant than ourselves. Let each of us look not only to our own interests, but also to the interests of others, having the very mind of Christ. Amen (Philippians 1 & 2).

*The true theology is warm, and it steams upward into prayer.*
~P.T. Forsyth

*H*ighly exalted God,

Please grow my beloved into a woman who does all things without grumbling or questioning, that she may be blameless and innocent, a child of God without blemish in the midst of a crooked and twisted generation. Let her shine as a light in the world, holding fast to the word of life, so that in the day of Christ I may be proud that I did not pray in vain or encourage her in vain. Enable me to rejoice and be glad to suffer for her sake—even to pour out my life as a drink offering upon the sacrificial offering of her faith. Likewise let her also be glad and rejoice with me to endure hardship for the name of Christ. Make her genuinely concerned for the welfare of others, seeking not her own interests but those of Jesus Christ.

O beloved, rejoice in the Lord. To say this same thing to you is no trouble to me and is safe for you. Look out for the dogs, look out for the evildoers, look out for those who put confidence in their works.

Father, help her to remain steadfast in worship by Your Spirit, glorying in Christ Jesus, and putting no confidence in the flesh. More than anything, strengthen her to forget what lies behind and strain forward to what lies ahead, and press on toward the goal for the prize of Your upward call in Christ Jesus. Let her also hold true to what she has attained. Amen (Philippians 2 & 3).

reat Savior,

Thank you that my wife's citizenship is in heaven! Therefore let her not set her mind on earthly things, but instead await a Savior, the Lord Jesus Christ, who will transform her lowly body to be like His glorious body, by the power that enables Him even to subject all things to Himself.

Therefore my beloved, whom I love and long for, my joy and crown, stand firm in the Lord. Rejoice in the Lord always; again I will say, Rejoice!

Father, teach her how to be content in every situation. Help her to know how to be brought low, and how to abound. In any and every circumstance show her the secret of facing plenty and hunger, abundance and need. Strengthen her to do all things through You. Please supply every need of hers according to Your riches in glory in Christ Jesus. To You, our God and Father, be glory forever and ever! May the grace of the Lord Jesus Christ be with her spirit. Amen (Philippians 3 & 4).

*When you encounter trial and suffering, what's the content of your prayer? If yours is primarily a plea for relief from suffering, then please know that this is biblical. It's certainly not unbiblical. We're encouraged by God in Scripture to pray for relief from suffering. But this should never be the exclusive focus of our prayers in those times.*
~C.J. Mahaney

$\mathcal{S}$overeign LORD of Zion,

Let my incomparable wife sing aloud and shout! May she rejoice and exult with all her heart as a daughter of Jerusalem. For You have taken away the judgments against her because of Christ. You have cleared away her enemies—death, sin, and Satan. Let her never again fear evil, for You—the King of Israel, the LORD—are near her.

May she not fear, and let not her hands grow weak.

O daughter of Zion, the LORD your God is with you, a mighty one who will save; He rejoices over you with gladness; He quiets you by His love; He exults over You with loud singing.

LORD God, when she mourns, please gather her and bring her to Your festival, so that she will no longer suffer reproach. Deal with all her oppressors. Change her shame into praise and renown in all the earth. Restore her fortunes so that You will be renowned and praised among all the peoples of the earth (Zephaniah 3).

*Restraining pray'r, we cease to fight;*
*Pray'r makes the Christian's armour bright.*
*~William Cowper*

$\mathcal{G}$od our Savior,

Thank You for Christ Jesus our hope. Watch over my splendid wife and guard her from those who teach any different doctrine, or devote themselves to myths, who promote speculations rather than the good order from You that is by faith. And as you protect her, fill her with the love that issues from a pure heart and a good conscience and a sincere faith. Let her not swerve from these, or wander away into vain discussion.

I thank You, Christ Jesus my Lord, for giving her strength, and because You judged her faithful, appointing her to Your service, though formerly she was so unworthy.

O beloved, rejoice! Remember that you received mercy, and the grace of our Lord overflowed for you with the faith and love that are in Christ Jesus.

I praise You, Father, for showing her mercy, so that in her Jesus Christ might display His perfect patience as an example to those who are to believe in Him for eternal life.

To You, the King of ages, immortal, invisible, the only God, be honor and glory forever and ever! Amen (I Timothy 1).

*There is nothing so abnormal, so unworldly, so supernatural, in human life as prayer.... The whole Christian life in so far as it is lived from the Cross and by the Cross is rationally an extravagance.* ~P.T. Forsyth

$\mathcal{M}$ighty LORD,

I entrust my peerless wife entirely to Your charge and care, in accordance with Your grace in Christ Jesus toward her. By Your power may she wage the good warfare, holding faith and a good conscience. Let her never make shipwreck of her faith!

Help me to be a man who prays without anger or quarreling. And continue to give her the wisdom and desire to adorn herself in respectable apparel, with modesty and self-control, not merely with braided hair and gold or pearls or costly attire, but with what is proper for women who profess godliness—with good works. Let her be the kind of woman who learns quietly with all submissiveness.

Protect her from those who depart from the faith by devoting themselves to deceitful spirits and teachings of demons. Let her have nothing to do with irreverent, silly myths. Rather train her for godliness, for while bodily training is of some value, godliness is of value in every way, as it holds promise for the present life and also for the life to come.

May she toil and strive to this end, because she has her hope set on You, the living God (I Timothy 1, 2, 4).

*If we do not abide in prayer, we shall abide in cursed temptations.*
~John Owen

$\mathcal{S}$avior of the weak,

Let my precious wife set an example for believers in speech, in conduct, in love, in faith, in purity.

Make her find full delight in the sound words of our Lord Jesus Christ and the teaching that accords with godliness. And keep her from an unhealthy craving for controversy and for quarrels about words. Let her instead pursue godliness with contentment, for therein there is great gain.

May she be content that she has food and clothing, and let her not desire to be rich.

O beloved, let us remind each other that those who desire to be rich fall into temptation, into a snare, into many senseless and harmful desires that plunge people into ruin and destruction.

Father, guard us from craving riches! For the love of money is the root of all kinds of evils. Keep us from the fate of those who, through this craving, have wandered away from the faith and pierced themselves with many pangs.

Let our love and craving be for Christ (I Timothy 4 & 6).

*For, as for my heart, when I go to pray, I find it so loth to go to God, and when it is with him, so loth to stay with him, that many times I am forced in my Prayers; first to beg God that he would take mine heart, and set it on himself in Christ, and when it is there, that he would keep it there (Psalm 86.11).* ~John Bunyan

$\mathcal{F}$ather of glory,

As for my pure wife, let her flee from the desire to be rich and the love of money. Help and enable her to pursue with renewed vigor righteousness, godliness, faith, love, steadfastness, and gentleness. Strengthen her to fight the good fight of the faith, and to take hold of the eternal life to which she was called.

O beloved, I charge you in the presence of God, who gives life to all things, and of Christ Jesus, to keep your conduct unstained and free from reproach until the appearing of our Lord Jesus Christ, which He will display at the proper time—He who is the blessed and only Sovereign, the King of kings and Lord of lords, who alone has immortality, who dwells in unapproachable light, whom no one has ever seen or can see.

To You, O God, be honor and eternal dominion! If You bless us with plenty, let us never become haughty or set our hopes on the uncertainty of riches. Rather cause us to set our hopes on You—the One who richly provides us with everything to enjoy. Help us together to do good, to be rich in good works, to be generous and ready to share, thus storing up treasure for ourselves as a good foundation for the future so that we may take hold of that which is truly life (I Timothy 6).

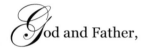od and Father,

May grace, mercy, and peace be multiplied to my dearest wife. I thank You as I remember her constantly in my prayers night and day. Thank You for granting me a woman who fills me with joy with each new sight of her. Please grow her faith in sincerity. Fan into flame the gifts You have given her, and remind her that You gave us a spirit not of fear but of power and love and self-control.

Therefore let her not be ashamed of the testimony about our Lord, but by Your power cause her to rejoice to share in suffering for the gospel. For You are the one who saved her and called us to a holy calling, not because of her works but because of Your own purpose and grace, which You gave her in Christ Jesus before the ages began. Thank You that He is her Savior, even He who abolished death and brought life and immortality to light through the gospel. Let her not be ashamed to suffer for this gospel, for she knows whom she has believed. Convince her that You are able to guard what has been entrusted to her until that Day.

O beloved, follow the pattern of the sound words that you have heard from the Scriptures, in the faith and love that are in Christ Jesus. By the Holy Spirit who dwells within us, guard the good deposit entrusted to you (II Timothy 1).

*It is not well for a man to pray cream and live skim milk.*
~Henry Ward Beecher

$\mathscr{F}$ather in heaven,

Please strengthen my beautiful wife by the grace that is in Christ Jesus, so that she may be able to share in suffering as His good soldier. May she constantly remember Jesus Christ, risen from the dead, the offspring of David. Let her rejoice to endure everything for the sake of the elect, that they also may obtain the salvation that is in Christ Jesus with eternal glory.

O beloved, the saying is trustworthy, for: If we have died with Him, we will also live with Him; if we endure, we will also reign with Him; if we deny Him, He also will deny us; if we are faithless, He remains faithful—for He cannot deny Himself.

O God, remind her of these things. Compel her to do her best to present herself to You as one approved, a worker who has no need to be ashamed, rightly handling the word of truth. May she avoid irreverent babble, for it will lead people into more and more ungodliness, and their talk will spread like gangrene. Thank You that Your firm foundation stands, bearing this seal: "The Lord knows those who are His," and "Let everyone who names the name of the Lord depart from iniquity" (II Timothy 2).

*Were it not for the Spirit, none would be able to persevere in prayer. 'A man without the help of the Spirit', John Bunyan once declared, 'cannot so much as pray once; much less, continue...in a sweet praying frame.' It needs to be noted that, for all who persevere in this struggle and discipline of prayer, there are times of exquisite delight when the struggle, and duty slides over into pure joy.* ~Michael A. G. Haykin

*H*oly Master,

Let my dear wife cleanse herself from what is dishonorable so that she will be a vessel for honorable use, set apart as holy, useful to You, ready for every good work.

Make her flee youthful passions and pursue righteousness, faith, love, and peace, along with those who call on the Lord from a pure heart. May she have nothing to do with foolish, ignorant controversies, since they breed quarrels. Let her not be quarrelsome but kind to everyone.

Help her to patiently endure evil. Protect her from those who are lovers of self, lovers of money, proud, arrogant, abusive, disobedient to their parents, ungrateful, unholy, heartless, unappeasable, slanderous, without self-control, brutal, not loving good, treacherous, reckless, swollen with conceit, lovers of pleasure rather than lovers of You, having the appearance of godliness, but denying its power. Help her to avoid such people.

Enable me to lead her righteously in my teaching, my conduct, my aim in life, my faith, my patience, my love, my steadfastness, and my persecutions and sufferings.

Indeed, beloved, let me remind you that all who desire to live a godly life in Christ Jesus will be persecuted, while evil people and imposters will go on from bad to worse, deceiving and being deceived.

But as for her, Lord God, may she continue in what she has learned and has firmly believed, becoming more and more acquainted with the sacred writings, which are able to make her wise for salvation through faith in Christ Jesus. Increase her love for Scripture. May what You have breathed out teach her, reprove her, correct her, and train her in righteousness, that she may be competent, equipped for every good work (II Timothy 2 & 3).

*My simple exhortation is this: Let us take time this very day to rethink our priorities and how prayer fits in. Make some new resolve. Try some new venture with God. Set a time. Set a place. Choose a portion of Scripture to guide you. Don't be tyrannized by the press of busy days. We all need midcourse corrections. Make this a day of turning to prayer—for the glory of God and for the fullness of your joy.*
~John Piper

$\mathscr{G}$od and Father of Christ Jesus,

who is to judge the living and the dead,

May my incomparable wife delight in and spread Your word all the more. Make her ready to bear witness to Christ's appearing and His kingdom in season and out of season. Let her reprove, rebuke, and exhort her sisters in Christ with complete patience and teaching.

Guard her from becoming a woman who will not endure sound teaching—one who, having itching ears, accumulates for herself teachers to suit her own passions, and turns away from listening to the truth and wanders off into myths. May it never be! Instead, keep her always sober-minded. Enable her to endure suffering, to do the work of an evangelist, and to fulfill the ministry to which You have called her.

O Father, please strengthen her to fight the good fight. Carry her onward to finish the race. Keep her so that she might keep the faith. Effect her heart to love Christ's appearing all the more, so that there may be laid up for her the crown of righteousness, which He, the righteous judge, will award to her on that Day.

May Christ Jesus and His grace be with her spirit. Amen (II Timothy 4).

*May God give us a heart and a will to make prayer,*
*prayer for the exaltation of God and extension of the kingdom,*
*a daily reality in our lives.* ~Michael A. G. Haykin

# *Appendix A*

## Books Quoted

Bounds, E.M. *Man of Prayer*
Bridges, Jerry. *Trusting God: Even When Life Hurts*
Brother Lawrence. *The Practice of the Presence of God*
Buttrick, George A. *Prayer*
Carson, D.A. *Call to Spiritual Reformation: Priorities from Paul and His Prayers*
Di Gangi, Marioano. *A Golden Treasury of Puritan Devotions*
Dubay, Thomas. *The Evidential Power of Beauty*
Edwards, Jonathan. *Religious Affections*
Edwards, Jonathan. *The Works of Jonathan Edwards, Vol. 2*
Forsyth, P.T. *The Soul of Prayer*
Grudem, Wayne. *Systematic Theology*
Haykin, Michael. *The God Who Draws Near*
Hosier, Helen. *Jonathan Edwards: The Great Awakener*
Mahaney, C.J. *Humility: True Greatness*
Mason, Mike. *Practicing the Presence of People*
Mason, Mike. *The Gospel According to Job*
Mason, Mike. *The Mystery of Marriage*
Merton, Thomas. *Contemplative Prayer*
Montgomery, L.M. *Emily Climbs*
Montgomery, L.M. *The Story Girl*
Mueller, George. *Autobiography of George Mueller*
Murray, Ian. *Jonathan Edwards: A New Biography*
Owen, John. *The Glory of Christ*
Packer, J.I. *Evangelism and the Sovereignty of God*
Piper, John, and Justin Taylor. *A God Entranced Vision of All Things*
Piper, John. *A Hunger for God: Desiring God Through Fasting and Prayer*
Piper, John. *Pierced by the Word*
Piper, John. *The Pleasures of God*
Piper, John. *The Roots of Endurance*
Piper, John. *What Jesus Demands from the World*
Spurgeon, Charles. *Lectures to My Students*
Torrey, R.A. *How to Pray*
Tozer, A. W. *God Tells the Man Who Cares*
Ware, Bruce. *God's Greater Glory*
Whitney, Donald. *Spiritual Disciplines for the Christian Life*
Whyte, Alexander. *Lord Teach Us to Pray*

# For Further Reading on the Subject of Prayer

Bennett, Arthur. *The Valley of Vision: Puritan Prayers and Devotions*
Calvin, John. *The Institutes of Christian Religion* (Book 3)
Carson, D.A. *Teach Us to Pray: Prayer in the Bible and the World*
Henry, Matthew. *A Method for Prayer*
Hunter, W. Bingham. *The God Who Hears*
Johnstone, Patrick, *Operation World: A day-to-day guide to praying for the world*
Owen, John. *Communion With God*
Palmer, B.M. *Theology of Prayer*
Piper, John. *Desiring God* (Chapter 6)
Piper, John. *When I Don't Desire God: How to Fight for Joy*
Pratt, Jr. Richard L. *Pray With Your Eyes Open*
Spurgeon, Charles. *Prayer and Spiritual Warfare*


# For Further Reading on the Subject of Marriage

Chapell, Bryan, and Kathy Chapell. *Each for the Other: Marriage As It's Meant to Be*
Greenwood, Glenn, and Latayne C. Scott. *A Marriage Made in Heaven*
Harvey, Dave. *When Sinners Say, "I Do"*
Köstenberger, Andreas J. *God, Marriage, and Family*
Lepine, Bob. *The Christian Husband*
Mahaney, C.J. *Sex, Romance, and the Glory of God: What Every Christian Husband Needs to Know*
Mason, Mike. *The Mystery of Marriage*
Piper, John. *This Momentary Marriage*
Priolo, Lou. *The Complete Husband*
Riccuci, Gary, and Betsy Riccuci. *Love That Lasts: When Marriage Meets Grace*
Wilson, Douglas. *Federal Husband*
Wilson, Douglas. *Fidelity: What It Means to Be a One-Woman Man*
Wilson, Douglas. *Reforming Marriage*

# *Appendix B*

## Prayers by Biblical Book & Chapter

# Notes:

2410971

Made in the USA